TURKEY
The Challenge of a New Role

THE WASHINGTON PAPERS

... intended to meet the need for an authoritative, yet prompt, public appraisal of the major developments in world affairs.

MANUSCRIPT SUBMISSION

The Washington Papers and Praeger Publishers welcome inquiries concerning manuscript submissions. Please include with your inquiry a curriculum vitae, synopsis, table of contents, and estimated manuscript length. Manuscript length must fall between 120 and 200 double-spaced typed pages. All submissions will be peer reviewed. Submissions to *The Washington Papers* should be sent to *The Washington Papers*; The Center for Strategic and International Studies; 1800 K Street NW; Suite 400; Washington, DC 20006. Book proposals should be sent to Praeger Publishers; 90 Post Road West; P.O. Box 5007; Westport, CT 06881-5007.

The Washington Papers/163

TURKEY
The Challenge of a New Role

Andrew Mango

Foreword by
Heath W. Lowry

PUBLISHED WITH
THE CENTER FOR STRATEGIC
AND INTERNATIONAL STUDIES
WASHINGTON, D.C.

PRAEGER

Westport, Connecticut
London

Library of Congress Cataloging-in-Publication Data

Mango, Andrew, 1926–
    Turkey : the challenge of a new role / Andrew Mango.
      p.   cm. – (Washington papers ; 163)
    "Published with the Center for Strategic and International
Studies, Washington, D.C."
    Includes bibliographical references and index.
    ISBN 0-275-94985-0 (alk. paper). – ISBN 0-275-94986-9 (pbk. :
alk. paper)
    1. Turkey – Politics and government – 1980– 2. Turkey – Foreign
relations – 1980– 3. Turkey – Social conditions – 1960– 4. Turkey –
Economic conditions – 1960– I. Center for Strategic &
International Studies (Washington, D.C.) II. Title. III. Series.
DR603.M36   1994
327.561 – dc20   94-10581

British Library Cataloging-in-Publication data is available.

Library of Congress Catalog Card Number: 94-10581
ISBN: 0-275-94985-0 (cloth)
      0-275-94986-9 (paper)

First published in 1994

Praeger Publishers, 88 Post Road West, Westport, CT 06881
An imprint of Greenwood Publishing Group, Inc.

Printed in the United States of America

∞™

The paper used in this book complies with the Permanent
Paper Standard issues by the National Information Standards
Organization (Z39.48-1984).

10 9 8 7 6 5 4 3 2 1

Contents

Foreword

To say that Andrew Mango's *Turkey: The Challenge of a New Role* provides a most welcome and timely addition to the nearly nonexistent monographic treatment of contemporary Turkey would be a gross understatement. His insightful analysis reflects both a close familiarity with and appreciation for the problems facing this key country.

Turkey is located in a neighborhood that by any standards must be termed marginal and in the wake of the collapse of the Soviet Union and the Warsaw Pact could well become a slum. Turkey's neighbors have traditionally included Iran, Iraq, Syria, Cyprus, Greece, Bulgaria, Romania, and the USSR; to this crowded list the USSR's collapse has added the Russian Republic, Moldova, Ukraine, Georgia, Armenia, and Azerbaijan.

Turkey is literally surrounded by instability. Russia, whose future is still to be determined, has recently begun exhibiting nationalist tendencies that do not bode well for Turkey. Georgia is still suffering the aftershocks of a particularly brutal civil war, and Armenia and Azerbaijan show little sign of resolving their five-year ethnic dispute over Nagorno-Karabakh. Iran, whose own future course is far from clear, spares no expense in exporting terrorism and its own brand of Islamic fundamentalism to neighboring Turkey. Iraq's future remains a question mark, and Syria (despite U.S. efforts to bring it back into the family of nations as part of the overall Arab-Israeli settlement) remains a major supporter of terrorism, much of it directed against Turkey. Greece, Turkey's long-time regional "ally" remains hostile over bilateral issues and the still unresolved Cyprus crisis. Not unlike a petulant child, it does what it can to destabilize Turkey—most recently allowing the terrorist Kurdish Workers' Party (PKK) to open offices in Athens. To survive in this version of the "new world order," Turkey needs a strong economy and a fair measure of internal stability.

Mango's perceptive study amply illustrates the absence of these factors in contemporary Turkey. He argues persuasively that Turkey's ability to play a more substantive role in its troubled part of the world is closely linked to its still undecided success in meeting its own growing internal problems, especially (1) a fragmented political system; (2) an economy stretched beyond its means by high inflation, mounting external and internal debt, and an outmoded tax system; and (3) the direct threat to its territorial integrity represented by the ever-mounting PKK insurgency in the southeast.

To this analysis must be added the growing tendency of an ever-increasing percentage of the electorate to reject the traditional political parties of the center-right and center-left in favor of extremist religious and ultra-nationalist alternatives on the radical right. This trend, observable in municipal and parliamentary election returns of the past five years, is startling: In the 1989 municipal elections, the extreme right took some 10.8 percent of the total vote (Welfare Party or RP 9.8 percent plus National Action Party or MHP 1.0 percent); two years later in the 1991 parliamentary elections, these two parties running together accounted for 16.9 percent of the nationwide total vote. On March 27, 1994, once again in municipal elections, the extreme right tallied 28.28 percent of the total (RP 18.99 percent plus MHP 8.03 percent plus BBP or Grand

Unity Party 1.26 percent). Stated differently, within the relatively short span of five years, that percentage of the electorate rejecting the traditional status quo has practically tripled and today comprises close to three out of every ten voters. Given the fragmentation of the Turkish political parties, a similar growth in the next two years could conceivably see the radical right emerge as the winner of the next scheduled parliamentary elections in 1996.

One thing is certain, as Mango writes, "Turkey and the West need each other as never before." His perceptive study can play a key role in drawing the attention of Western policymakers to this all-important truth. It behooves us all to focus less on what is wrong with Turkey today than on a far more important question: How can the West help ensure that the only Muslim democracy surmounts its current problems and reemerges as strengthened proof that Islam and democracy are not incompatible? Andrew Mango has set forth the problems. Now all of us must look for ways to resolve them.

Heath W. Lowry
Atatürk Professor of Ottoman
and Modern Turkish Studies
Princeton University

About the Author

Andrew Mango was for 14 years in charge of broadcasts in Turkish for the British Broadcasting Corporation (BBC), later heading the BBC's South European Service and its French Language Service. The former publisher of *Turkey Confidential*, a monthly newsletter on Turkish affairs, Dr. Mango is an honorary research associate of the Modern Turkish Studies Program at the University of London. He served as a member of the editorial board for the Turkish edition of the *Encyclopaedia Britannica*.

Dr. Mango visits Turkey several times a year for academic purposes or journalistic assignments. He was born in Istanbul in 1926 and educated there at the English High School. In 1955 he received his Ph.D. from the School of Oriental and African Studies, University of London, where he complemented his knowledge of Turkish by reading Persian and Arabic. Dr. Mango's books include *Turkey* (1968), *Discovering Turkey* (1971), and *Turkey: A Delicately Poised Ally* (1975). His articles on Turkey and the Middle East have appeared in *Middle Eastern Studies* and numerous other journals and books.

Summary

The republic of Turkey has matured into a middle-ranking regional power. Founded in 1923 by Mustafa Kemal (Atatürk) as the central successor state of the Ottoman Empire, it is ruled by a freely elected parliament and pursues economic development within the global free market system. Its tradition of statecraft, inherited from the old empire, has helped it surmount internal political crises and develop a successful foreign policy that has ensured the support of like-minded foreign powers in defense of Turkish national independence and the general world order.

When Andrew Mango wrote his first Washington Paper on Turkey in 1975 (*Turkey: A Delicately Poised Ally*), internal tensions were threatening to erupt into full-scale civil war between Marxists and nationalists, and the country's membership in the North Atlantic Treaty Organization was being challenged by a vocal body of neutralists. Both dangers were averted, and Turkey successfully discharged its role as southeastern bastion of the Western alliance until the cold war's end brought disintegration to the Warsaw Pact and the Soviet Union.

From the Truman Doctrine's inception in March 1947 until the end of the cold war, Western — especially U.S. — aid to Turkey was firmly grounded in common interests. It succeeded in its aim of keeping Turkey out of the reach communist predators and ensuring Turkey's democratic and economic development. Today there is a new common interest in creating a stable, free order in the former communist countries and in the Middle East. Turkey's leaders claim that their country can promote this interest in cooperation with the West and other advanced industrial countries. In particular, they point to Turkey's unique distinction as a secular Muslim country that governs itself by a freely elected parliament, applies free market economic policies at home, and continues its long tradition of cooperating with Western democracies abroad. In addition, they claim a special relationship with the Turkic republics of the former Soviet Union, as well as a fund of knowledge in dealing with the problems of neighboring countries in the Balkans, the Black Sea region, and the Middle East.

By siding unequivocally with the U.S.-led coalition that ejected Saddam Hussein's forces from Kuwait, the late president Turgut Özal (d. 1993) showed that Turkey could contribute to establishing order in its vicinity. Its ability to do so in the Balkans, the Black Sea area, and the southern part of the former Soviet Union depends both on external factors and on Turkey's own internal strength and cohesion. The latter is threatened by the rise of Kurdish nationalism, manifested today in the terrorist campaign of the Kurdish Workers' Party (PKK), and by populist economic policies that have ensured consumer-led growth at the cost of high inflation. The Turkish economy is strained by the effort of satisfying the high material expectations of the electorate, and the Turkish government has yet to work out how to satisfy the aspirations of its Kurdish citizens within a unitary, democratic structure. Although the persistence of these internal problems and of the continuing tensions produced by rapid demographic growth and urbanization limits Turkish ability to affect events abroad, Turkey can still function constructively as a regional role model, backed by its real achievements and more directly by its economic enterprise and such economic and technical aid as it can provide.

Turkey will increase its ability to play a regional role as it progresses toward integration in the global economy — an effort that includes the goal of full membership in the European Union, formerly the European Community — and as it finds solutions to its internal problems. Given that this role serves general Western interests as it did during the cold war, the West will find it useful to continue supporting Turkey's economic development and showing understanding for its internal political problems, while making clear its own preference for democratic solutions.

This interpretation of both Turkey's position and the proper Western response to it is bound to be challenged by the country's ethnic adversaries. But the latter misunderstand Turkey's real goals and exaggerate its ambitions. Atatürk's aim to "reach the level of contemporary [Western] civilization" continues to be shared by the vast majority of Turkish citizens today, who mainly aspire to the material standards prevailing in the advanced industrialized countries. Rapid material development — not irredentism — is the mainspring of Turkish politics; claims to regional influence and attempts to exercise it are thus mainly inspired by the hope of attracting the investment and general support of Western and other advanced industrialized countries. If a gap exists today between Turkey's claims to regional influence and its material means to exercise it, Turks hope that their foreign friends will help to narrow it by choosing them as their partners. This hope deserves the sympathetic attention of the West.

Note on Turkish
Spelling and Pronunciation

Turkish uses the Latin alphabet. Letter are pronounced as in English (or Spanish in the case of vowels), except that

c is pronounced as *j* in *jet*
ç is pronounced as *ch* in *church*
g is always hard as in *go*
ğ is silent, but lengthens the preceding vowel
ı (without a dot) is similar to the sound in Slavic languages represented (in Polish) by *y*. The nearest English equivalent would be the phantom vowel between *b* and *l* in *marble*.
j is pronounced as in French, or like *s* in *measure*.
ö is pronounced as in German, or like *eu* in the French word *peur*
ş is pronounced as *sh* in *ship*
ü is pronounced as in German or like *u* in the French word *pur*.

Introduction

The republic of Turkey celebrated its seventieth birthday on October 29, 1993. Its founding after World War I went against the wishes of the victors, but accorded with the principle of national self-determination proclaimed by the Allies as one of their war aims. Of all the new states formed at the time, Turkey has had the most untroubled existence – enjoying peace for 70 years as its people increased fivefold and improved their lot. Today the 60 million citizens of the Turkish republic live longer; are better fed, housed, and clothed; and enjoy more freedom than did the 12 million original inhabitants of the republic.

Still, the aim of Mustafa Kemal Atatürk, the founding father of the republic, is yet to be realized. He wanted Turkey to reach "the level of contemporary civilization" – the level, in other words, of the most advanced countries of the world. Today Turkey is indeed a member of the club of rich countries, the Organization for Economic Cooperation and Development (OECD). But even though its population accounts for 7 percent of the total population of OECD member states, its gross national product is valued at only 1.3 percent of the OECD total. All indicators of living standards put Turkey at the bottom of the OECD league.

Turkey's record could hardly have been otherwise; in-

1

deed, it could have been much worse, given the country's backwardness 70 years ago. Although the perception of relative disadvantage, of pressing and seemingly increasing problems, and of the difficulties of daily life weigh on the feelings of the citizens of the 70-year-old republic, outside observers should be in a better position to see the scale of Turkey's achievements.

The West has particular reason to be thankful for the Turkish republic. During the long years of the cold war, Turkey served as the southeastern bastion of the North Atlantic Treaty Organization (NATO), helping to prevent a Soviet breakthrough to the south. Today, Turkey is still an island of relative stability in a stormy sea lapping round the walls of fortress Europe and threatening prosperous countries everywhere. But the situation raises questions: how stable is Turkey is itself; if it is indeed stable, how capable is it of spreading stability around it?

The West, expecially the United States, should not lack knowledge on which to base an answer. Since Turkey began to receive U.S. aid under the Truman Doctrine in March 1947, thousands of Americans have visited Turkey, served there, advised Turks, done business with them, studied their country. Recent literature on Turkey is indeed both extensive and impressive, as scholars have made good use of the open access the country affords.

Yet the spread of this knowledge to the wider Western public has meant contending with extraneous difficulties. The Turkish nation state was born of a bloody process— the slow and painful disintegration of the Ottoman Empire. The Christian West saw it as a process of emancipation of downtrodden Christian peoples from the misrule of Muslim Turkish oppressors. More recently historians have qualified this impression by pointing both to the virtues of Ottoman rule and to the sufferings of the Muslims when that rule ended. Their findings have been graphically confirmed by current events in the former Yugoslavia as well as by recent events in Lebanon. Today it should be easier to accept the conclusion reached by Professor Justin McCarthy

in his study of Muslims, Greeks, and Armenians in Otto-
man Anatolia (Asia Minor) at the end of the empire: "Both
Muslims and Christians were killers, both Muslims and
Christians were killed."[1]

Nevertheless, the wrongs suffered in the past by
Greeks and Armenians in particular, rather than the
wrongs suffered by the Turks, continue to affect percep-
tions of modern Turkey. Moreover, national prejudice overlaps with ideological prejudice. The Ottoman Empire, naturally enough, drew the fire of liberal revolutionaries. But
the perception of all Turks as right-wing conservatives sur-
vived the founding of the modern Turkish republic to re-
emerge when that republic allied itself with the United
States in the cold war. Liberals who view it as axiomatic
that "America has been willing to tolerate harsh dictatorship in the interest of what is sometimes cynically described as stability" see in Turkey's alliance with the
United States the mark of Cain.[2]

Thus the sufferings are recounted of the Armenians
(but not of the Turks) in World War I, of the Greeks in
Cyprus in 1974 (but not of Cypriot Turks between 1963 and
1974), of today's Kurds (but not of the victims of Kurdish
terrorism). Such retelling combines with accusations of violations of human rights to distort the Western perception
of Turkey.

To understand Turkey requires acknowledging two
facts: most Turks share the Western aspiration to a free
and comfortable life, and the governments they elect must
seek to meet this aspiration. This perception of the national interest colors Turkey's foreign policy. It is pru-
dently averse to foreign adventures. It seeks out common
interests with like-minded allies. As Margaret Thatcher
once said with reference to Mikhail Gorbachev, Turkey is a
country with which one can do business.

In its internal affairs, Turkey is trying to cope with
the effects of a demographic explosion and burgeoning expectations. When the populations of West European countries increased rapidly in the last century, the New World

afforded space and scope for energies that could not be absorbed at home. Today no empty spaces are left in the world, and Turks who seek their fortunes abroad are not honored as pioneers, but reviled as unwanted, and often illegal, foreign workers.

In many countries that have now achieved the comfort of stability, the process of nation building, the passing of a traditional society, the advent of industry, and the process of urbanization were all attended by social convulsions that led occasionally to civil war. In the republic of Turkey, where change has been and continues to be both rapid and uncomfortable, civil conflict has so far been contained — thanks largely to Turkey's experience of statecraft inherited from the Ottoman Empire.

In its 70 years, Turkey has seen two military coups and one more limited military intervention. But the three military interludes, taken together, add up to less time than the seven years Greece was ruled by the Colonels' regime (1967–1974), a period ended only by the pressure of external forces. In Turkey, moderates have consistently proved stronger than radicals, and the development of stable democratic institutions, although seconded by the West, has relied largely on internal dynamics.

Turkey is not yet out of the woods. But is any other country in that vast region stretching between the European Union (formerly the European Community) and the Pacific Rim? Stability is relative, and critics who point to Turkey's weaknesses would do well to think whether there is any more stable country that could serve as a support of world order in the region.

1

The Maturing of a Nation-State

The republic of Turkey is the central successor state
of the multinational, or rather multiconfessional, Ottoman
Empire, which, at the time of its maximum expansion in
the sixteenth century, stretched from the gates of Vienna
to the Indian Ocean and from the steppes of southern Russia to the Sahara desert. The Ottoman Empire was founded
by Turks whose origin lay in central Asia. The Turks began
their conquest of the Christian lands of the Eastern Roman
(Byzantine) Empire in 1071, when they defeated the emperor Romanos IV Diogenes at Malazgirt in what is now
eastern Turkey. In 1453, the Byzantine capital, Constanti-
nople, fell to Sultan Mehmet II, named the Conqueror. By
that time, the Ottomans had penetrated deep into eastern
Europe.

The advance into Europe had started in the middle of
the fourteenth century; it ended with the failure of the
second siege of Vienna in 1683. The retreat to the present
frontiers of the Turkish republic took more than two centuries, allowing the Ottomans ample time to leave their imprint on the Balkans. In the Arab lands of the Middle East,
Ottoman rule lasted from the beginning of the sixteenth
to the beginning of the twentieth centuries. There too it
profoundly influenced society.

5

The Ottoman Empire was organized according to Islamic principles. Non-Muslims who submitted to Muslim rule were given protected status and were allowed to run their own communal affairs. Forcible conversion to Islam was banned in theory and rare in practice, because it diminished the yield of taxes levied on non-Muslims. The one exception, an Ottoman innovation, was the Janissary corps based on the forcible recruitment and conversion to Islam of Christian boys largely from the Balkans. As members of the corps rose to the highest positions in the sultan's service, recruiting sergeants did not always have to rely on coercion.

Evidence suggests that mass conversions to Islam (in the regions of Bosnia, Albania, and the eastern Black Sea coast) occurred voluntarily among formerly disaffected subjects of Christian rulers. The number of Muslims also grew as the result of a rule that banned marriages between non-Muslim men and Muslim women, but allowed Muslim men to marry non-Muslim women. The children of these marriages were brought up as Muslims.

Muslims formed the majority in Anatolia, probably from the fourteenth century onward, and Christians had an overall majority in the Balkans. But Muslims and non-Muslims were to be found everywhere, given that the Ottomans were more tolerant of religious diversity than were contemporary Christian rulers. Non-Muslims dominated trade, the professions, and crafts. Their power and influence increased as the empire began its slow decline at the end of the seventeenth century. Increasing economic and social power fed demands for political emancipation, demands supported by the Christian great powers.

When the Ottomans lost their outlying provinces to their two Christian neighbors, Russia and the Hapsburg Empire, many Muslims were expelled while others fled. Then, through the nineteenth century, Christians in the Balkans rose up against their Ottoman rulers and founded their own national states. This was seen in the West as a process of emancipation. In fact, although the reforms that the sultans introduced at the prompting of the Christian great powers did bring a measure of political emancipation to non-Muslims in the remaining Ottoman dominions, the Christian successor states in the Balkans were born of a process known today as ethnic cleansing.

All the local Muslims fled or were killed when the original kingdom of Greece was formed in 1830. The same happened when Serbia first became independent. As the kingdom of Montenegro expanded, Muslims were thrown out of their homes. The number of Muslims declined rapidly in Romania. Bulgaria's proportion of Muslims—roughly half of the population—was reduced by mass killings, expulsion, and flight.

Greece, the first independent nation-state carved out of a multinational empire, was a product of the European ideology of nationalism grafted onto a confessional community. The modernizing elite of the Ottoman Empire tried to stem the nationalism of subject peoples with the ideology of Ottoman patriotism. When this failed, Turkish nationalism arose as a defensive ideology. It gathered strength when the empire lost almost all its remaining possessions in Europe during the Balkan wars of 1912–1913. It triumphed after the loss of the Arab provinces in World War I and the defeat of the Greek invasion of Anatolia in its aftermath.

The victorious Allies, who had espoused emancipation for the Christian, then theoretically the Arab, and conditionally the Kurdish subjects of the sultans, sought to deny it to the Turks. The attempt failed because of the resistance of the Muslim people of Anatolia, organized by Mustafa Kemal, an Ottoman general born in Salonika, who first made his name defending Gallipoli in 1915. As a result of the victory of Turkish nationalists led by Mustafa Kemal in the War of Independence, the Treaty of Sèvres, signed in 1920 with the intention of partitioning the Turkish core of the Ottoman Empire, was replaced in 1923 by the Treaty of Lausanne, which established the frontiers of the independent Turkish state.

On October 29, 1923, the Grand National Assembly, which had come together during the War of Independence to represent the sovereign rights of Ottoman Muslims in Thrace and Anatolia, proclaimed the Turkish Republic. An internationally recognized Turkish nation-state was thus born. Mustafa Kemal was its first president and its autocratic ruler until his death on November 10, 1938. In 1934, the assembly gave him the surname of Atatürk (Father of the Turks), at a time when all citizens of the republic (who were earlier known by their Muslim forenames and patronymics) were required to choose surnames.

The Turkish Republic has been molded by Atatürk's inspiration. His aim was to bring "contemporary civilization" to Turkey, and although he preferred not to call it Western civilization, he followed the Ottoman reformers of the nineteenth century in drawing his inspiration from the West in general and France in particular.

A man of the Enlightenment, Atatürk saw in religion a retrograde force, although he had used religious sentiment to mobilize his people in the War of Independence. He was also a modern man, who realized the importance of economic development. He was pragmatic in drawing on several models, as circumstances required. Not only Western democracy but fascist authoritarianism and Soviet practice influenced the early development of the republic. The title of the first republican cabinet was a Turkish translation of "Committee of Executive Commissars." Fascist corporatism served as a model when the public sector of the Turkish economy was promoted in the 1930s. But Atatürk always adhered to the forms of parliamentary democracy and used its discourse.

Atatürk's main legacy has been his adoption of nationalist secularism as the official ideology of the republic. After the last sultan, who had sided with the Allies in the War of Independence, had fled and the republic was proclaimed, a member of the Ottoman dynasty was allowed to exercise the function of spiritual caliph under the authority of the National Assembly. This historical anomaly ended in 1924, when the caliph was exiled together with all members of the Ottoman dynasty.

In the following 10 years, religious courts and schools were abolished and religious brotherhoods banned; first international numerals and then the Latin alphabet were adopted to replace the Arabic script; civil, commercial, and penal codes were imported from Switzerland, Germany, and Italy; the international (Christian) calendar was introduced with Sunday as a day of rest; and specifically Eastern and religious forms of dress were banned, as were traditional titles. In 1934 women were given the right to vote and be elected. Nationalist ideology inspired the elimination of as many Arabic and Persian words as possible from the Turkish language and the rewriting of history to stress the Turkish contribution to civilization.

Although they appeared revolutionary at the time, most of these measures were the logical culmination of Ottoman reforms undertaken in the nineteenth century and under the Young Turks after 1908. The Ottoman reformers aimed at a Western-style centralized state; Atatürk actually established it. His reforms had the support of the majority of educated Turks, who had been trained in similar ideals. Kemalism (Turks call it Atatürkism) was quickly adopted as the ideology of military officers and public servants.

Today, although some aspects of the reforms remain controversial, support for them extends beyond the armed forces and the elite to wide strata of society. True, there have been some adjustments (see chapter 5), but some of these affect details of, or later additions to, the canon. The veiling of women was thus discouraged, rather than prohibited, except among civil servants; penalties for reciting the call to prayer in Arabic rather than Turkish were imposed only after Atatürk's death — a fact that made it easier to revert to Arabic after World War II.

One feature of Turkish society that Atatürk left unchanged was the tradition of state paternalism, not to say authoritarianism. Although he declared that "the peasant is our master," the peasant did, and was conditioned to do, as he was told.

In the War of Independence, Mustafa Kemal realized almost all his territorial aims. The one exception was the oil-rich province of Mosul, which had been occupied by British troops after the conclusion of the armistice in 1918. In 1926, Turkey recognized it as part of the new kingdom of Iraq, which was then under British mandate. In 1939, a few months after Atatürk's death, France ceded to Turkey the province of Alexandretta (Iskenderun), which had a mixed Turkish-Arab population and was administered separately within French-mandated Syria. It became the Turkish province of Hatay.

As a territorially contented state, the republic of Turkey has sided with defenders of the status quo throughout its history. Between World Wars I and II, the status quo was threatened by Fascist Italy and then by Nazi Germany. After World War II, the threat came from the Communist Soviet Union. Turkish diplomacy, as inspired by Atatürk and molded by his main lieutenant and successor Ismet Inönü, sought to parry the threat by adopting a firm defensive posture and seeking like-minded allies.

In the 1930s, Turkey entered into limited and ineffective defensive alliances with its Balkan neighbors to the west and its Muslim neighbors to the east. These arrangements seconded the Anglo-French strategy of containing the Nazi-Fascist threat, a strategy that foundered on the Molotov-Ribbentrop Pact.

The pact created a new situation for Turkey too. Lenin had supported Turkish nationalists in their War of Independence, seeing them as the enemies of his enemies — Britain and the other "interventionists." Thereafter, relations between Turkey and the Soviet Union remained good or at least correct until 1939, when Stalin made clear his ambition to control the Turkish Straits. Nevertheless, when Turkey signed in that year an alliance with France and

Britain, it stipulated that its action would not be directed against the Soviet Union.

In any event, Ismet Inönü kept Turkey neutral until 1944, when he broke off relations with Germany. A purely formal declaration of war followed in February 1945, allowing Turkey to become a founding member of the United Nations (UN).

Certainly from 1942 onward, Inönü saw that the main threat to his country came from Stalin's Russia. As he resisted the demands of Winston Churchill and the other Allied leaders for Turkey to enter the war against Germany, he looked forward to the day when the wartime alliance would split and the West would need Turkey as a barrier to Soviet encroachment.

That day came in March 1947 when the Truman Doctrine committed the United States to the defense of Greece and Turkey. U.S. military aid was supplemented by economic aid, as Turkey became a beneficiary of the Marshall Plan. In 1950, Turkey contributed a brigade to the U.S.-led UN forces, which succeeded in stopping communist aggression in Korea. This decision, and the distinguished war record of Turkish troops in Korea, helped Turkey realize its aim of joining the North Atlantic Treaty Organization (NATO), to which it was admitted in 1952.

For more than 40 years, the American alliance has been the cornerstone of Turkish foreign policy and has also affected the course of Turkish domestic politics. The alliance was sometimes strained by problems that gradually defined its scope; it was at times controversial (in both countries). But the persistence of common interests has ensured its survival.

The main domestic effect of the U.S. alliance, and of Turkey's membership in NATO, has been to promote the development of parliamentary democracy. Atatürk ruled the country autocratically through the Republican People's Party (RPP), which he founded. During two brief intervals, he allowed opposition parties to function. But it was not until Turkey joined the U.S.-led Western alliance after World War II that free multiparty politics could develop.

The first genuinely free elections in the history of the republic were held in 1950, when the RPP, led by Atatürk's successor Inönü, was defeated and replaced in power by the Democrat Party (DP). The Democrat leadership, including the new president Celal Bayar and the new prime minister Adnan Menderes had started their political careers in the ranks of the RPP. They differed from their old party in being more liberal in their economic policies and more conservative in their cultural policies.

The main change after 1950, however, was not the slow and faltering move to a free market or the provision of greater state financial support for the practice of Islam. The big change in 1950 was the advent of electoral power. Until then, insofar as the ordinary citizen was concerned, power had been vested in the civil and military bureaucracy and in the single party, which overlapped with it. The provincial governor, district officer, local commander, tax collector, policeman and gendarme had ruled the land. After 1950, their power was circumscribed. Political parties and, in the first place, the ruling Democrat Party, became an alternative source of power. Civil servants could be challenged, sometimes transferred (or, more rarely, dismissed) as a result of political pressure. They did not relish the change. Neither did the old republican establishment, which had controlled the state and whose livelihood depended largely on state power and patronage. The class, or rather caste, of secularized intellectuals, who had grown up under the single-party regime and voiced its philosophy, was at the heart of that establishment.

The secular elite was, or believed itself to be, in favor of liberal democracy. Before and immediately after the elections of 1950, many members supported the DP. But it soon became clear to them that electoral power threatened their material interests and their way of life. After the Democrats were reelected with an increased majority in 1954, the universities and the press became the focus of opposition. The elite complained that Atatürk's secularism was being whittled down, even though under the Democrats Atatürk's remains were transferred to a grandiose mausoleum in Ankara and a law was passed to protect Atatürk's memory (in response to an emerging Muslim dervish order, whose members mutilated the ubiquitous busts of Atatürk). Yet the complaints of the secularists threatened the Democrats only when added to economic grievances.

The DP's accession to power inaugurated a period of rapid economic development, releasing productive energies earlier restrained by the state. A combination of factors — U.S. aid, the advent of mechanized farming, the construction of roads and dams, and the effect of the Korean War in raising the prices of, and increasing demand for, Turkey's agricultural products — considerably raised the standard of living of citizens throughout the country and even more dramatically affected their expectations. Towns grew prosperous, while villages emerged from abject poverty. But, inevitably, economic progress could not keep up with popular expectations. Equally inevitably, in conditions of electoral competition, the ruling Democrats forced the pace of development, causing inflation and straining the patience of U.S. aid officials and, more seriously, of foreign creditors, on whom Turkey had to rely to finance government overspending.

Moreover, there were losers as well as winners. Inflation hit salary-earners, especially the civilians and the military on the public payroll. They suffered a loss of esteem, first from political change, then from their relative economic impoverishment. The observation that in the late 1950s army officers could only afford the cheapest soft drinks when they went out became part of folklore.

Faced with discontent in different quarters, the ruling Democrats changed the electoral law. By banning electoral coalitions, they set a precedent that has been followed to this day. Changing the rules of the game before each electoral contest has become an unchanging rule of Turkish politics.

In 1957, the Democrats won their third election and kept their majority in parliament, although their share in the polls dropped from 57 percent to 48 percent. It was a Pyrrhic victory. As Ismet Inönü led the RPP in a vigorous countrywide campaign, the government took fright and granted extraordinary powers to a commission, made up of its supporters in parliament, to investigate the activities of the opposition. University students and then, more ominously, young officers and military cadets took to the streets. Sensing the support of the educated elite, military conspirators swung into action. The conspirators were mainly radical middle-ranking officers, who merged their differences in a common allegiance to Atatürk's reforms. At the last moment, they obtained the support of a senior officer, General Cemal Gürsel, who had retired from the command of the land forces after a disagreement with the government.

On May 27, 1960, the military took over the government in a bloodless coup—the first in the history of the republic. The entire parliamentary group of the DP was put on trial by the new military rulers. They called themselves the National Unity Committee (NUC), which was headed by General Gürsel, the new head of state. As the trials proceeded and an appointed constituent assembly drew up a new constitution, differences developed within the NUC. It is difficult to attach ideological labels to the various contending military factions, particularly as the tension between them was fed by personal antagonisms and ambitions. Age and rank were also factors in the conflict.

Soon after the coup, however, two broad tendencies emerged. Some members of the NUC, including General Gürsel, favored a speedy return to civilian parliamentary rule. The second tendency was more authoritarian. Some of the younger and more junior officers wanted to stay in power to carry out "reforms" to safeguard and then push forward the work of Atatürk. The "reformers" tended to be nationalists who had seized on such fashionable ideas as land reform, social justice, and egalitarianism. Whatever the ideas, they wanted to impose them on the country. Later some of the reformers were to flirt with national Marxism, while others moved into extreme right-wing politics. The proponents of authoritarian solutions were defeated by the more pragmatic group around General Gürsel, although the advocacy of ill-defined radical solutions to the country's problems continued to bedevil Turkish politics for many years to come.

Moderation did not win an unqualified victory in the contests and arguments that followed the 1960 coup. The deposed prime minister Adnan Menderes and his ministers of foreign affairs and finance were hanged at the close of what was clearly a political trial. This left a scar that took 30 years to heal. Finally, on September 17, 1990, in a state ceremony led by President Turgut Özal, the remains of the three hanged politicians, now known as "martyrs of democracy," were reinterred in a mausoleum in Istanbul.

The authors of the 1960 coup claimed that they were themselves defending democracy against an elected dictatorship. Once the authoritarian reformers had been removed, a democratic constitution was in fact drafted and approved in the 1961 referendum. It sought to circumscribe the powers of the elected majority in parliament by instituting a second chamber and a constitutional court and by proclaiming the autonomy of universities, broadcasting, and other institutions. It also wrote out a check that no government could honor, proclaiming all manner of social and economic rights, such as work, housing, education, and social welfare.

Thus, paradoxically, the 1960 military coup ushered in a period of free political debate such as Turkey had never seen. But it was also a period of recurrent instability.

Under the new constitution, free elections were held on October 15, 1961. The Democrat Party had earlier been dissolved and its constituency split between two parties, of which the Justice Party was the stronger. The split allowed Inönü's Republican People's Party to win the plurality. Inönü thus became prime minister at the head of unstable coalitions, with Cemal Gürsel now civilian president of the republic.

Inönü served the country well by opposing his authority against two attempted military coups. Because Inönü represented both democratic and Kemalist legitimacy, military revolutionaries could not subvert the majority of commanders in key positions. Gradually, hierarchical order was reestablished in the armed forces. But there were still proponents of a left-wing military dictatorship (on the lines of the authoritarian governments formed by the Arab Ba'th party). Although Marxist political activity remained theoretically banned in Turkey until 1991, various Marxist solutions to the country's problems were openly advocated in the wake of the 1961 elections. From the universities and the media, Marxist influence spread to active politics. Inönü tried to meet it by moving his party to the left, thus cutting the ground under the feet of the new, Marxist Turkish Workers' Party.

Among the many varieties of Turkish Marxism, nationalist Marxism or Marxist nationalism has been the most enduring. It still survives under the guise of anti-imperialism, where it overlaps with radical right-wing politics.

Inönü was in power when the Turkish community in the newly independent republic of Cyprus was attacked by Greek Cypriots in December 1963. When Turkish diplomatic initiatives failed to redress the situation, Inönü informed U.S. ambassador Raymond Hare on June 4, 1964, that he had decided to intervene militarily in Cyprus. On the following day, he was handed a reply from U.S. President Lyndon Johnson, who rejected the argument that peaceful means had been exhausted and included this threat: "I hope that you will understand that your NATO allies have not had a chance to consider whether they have an obligation to protect Turkey against the Soviet Union if Turkey takes a step which results in Soviet intervention without the full consent and understanding of its NATO allies."[3]

The Johnson letter averted a Turkish landing in Cyprus, at the cost of fueling anti-American sentiment in Turkey. Even more important was its influence on Turkish foreign policy. It did not destroy the alliance with the United States as the cornerstone of Turkish diplomacy. But it showed that Turkish national interests were not coterminous with NATO interests and that where the two diverged, Turkey had to look after itself. Until 1964, friction between Turkey and the United States had arisen mainly over the amount of U.S. aid. After the Johnson letter, political grievances began to complicate the relationship.

Under Inönü's leadership, relations with the Soviet Union began to improve, attempts were made to court Arab support, and Turkey became an associate member of the European Community or EC. (After November 1, 1993, the European Community became known as the European Union under the Maastricht Treaty.) But his coalition government fell apart a few months before the general elections of October 1965. Inönü's decision to reposition his party to the left of center did not prevent, and may even have accelerated, his defeat at the hands of Suleyman Demirel, the new leader of the Justice Party, who succeeded in reuniting the old constitutency of the Democrat Party.

Demirel entered politics in 1962 at the age of 38. Elected leader of the Justice Party in November 1964, he became deputy prime minister in February of the following year and prime minister eight months later. He has thus been a leading player on the Turkish political stage for more than 30 years. His record shows him to be a skillful tactician and a supple conciliator, a patient politician trying to avoid painful choices in the hope that problems will eventually solve themselves. His guiding principle has been the supremacy of civil power and respect for the letter of constitutional legality. He has been shaped in domestic conflict with the military and their civilian allies.

Demirel is, of course, a nationalist, but in the nonirredentist tradition of Atatürk and Inönü. At home he is wedded to the "one country, one nation" principle of Kemalism, which is currently under attack from Kurdish nationalists.

Demirel's peasant origin and reliance on electoral support have helped make him a "development politician," aiming at the delivery of services to an electorate avid for material improvements. Although neither an ideologist nor a visionary, he, like other development politicians, wants to leave his mark on the country in the shape of impressive public works. Demirel is not afraid of foreign debt. "Debt is the brave man's spur" is one of his best-known aphorisms. Others he has used include "Yesterday was different" (when defending himself against the charge of inconsistency), and "Don't worry, the streets won't wear out" (when urged to take action against demonstrators).

Demirel inherited the Cyprus problem when he first assumed office. In 1967, he threatened a military intervention when two Turkish Cypriot villages were overrun by the Greeks. But he went along with the U.S. mediator Cyrus Vance, and the crisis was solved, largely to Turkey's advantage. Mainland Greek troops smuggled into the island were withdrawn, and the blockade of Turkish Cypriots was relaxed.

In 1968, a wave of student militancy moved quickly from France to Turkey, where it split into two antagonistic camps—extreme nationalists and Marxist revolutionaries. The former organized themselves into "Idealist Hearths" (whose members were known as Grey Wolves) and the latter into "Revolutionary Youth" (Dev-Genç), which in turn split into "Revolutionary Left" (Dev-Sol) and "Revolutionary Path" (Dev-Yol). To this day, Dev-Sol is the main non-ethnic terrorist organization active in Turkey.

An Islamic party, the National Order Party (later the National Salvation Party), which had emerged under Professor Necmettin Erbakan, profited from the latitude allowed by the 1961 constitution and formed its own militant youth organization, known as the Raiders (Akıncılar).

Anti-American demonstrations by leftist militants and clashes between leftist and rightist militants spread beyond university campuses. By 1971, the kidnapping of a U.S. sergeant and four NATO radar technicians marked the degeneration of student militancy into terrorism. Because Demirel's government was weakened by a split within the Justice Party and was unable to find common ground on the security question with the opposition RPP, the high command of the armed forces imposed a national government under an elder statesman, Professor Nihat Erim. Both major parties agreed to cooperate, although within the RPP the decision was criticized by the secretary general Bülent Ecevit, who had championed the party's move to the left. Ecevit challenged the party's aging leader Inönü and succeeded in replacing him in 1972.

The "coup by memorandum," as the military intervention of March 12, 1971, came to be known, was followed by the imposition of martial law and constitutional amendments. Islamic and Marxist parties were closed down, and widespread arrests and trials (followed by the execution of three student militants) ensured a temporary restoration of order, but not before the Israeli consul general in Istanbul and three NATO radar technicians had been murdered. Faced with the beginnings of Kurdish nationalist militancy, the military obtained parliamentary approval to curtail constitutional freedoms when the integrity of the country was threatened.

Parliament constantly forced changes in the military-backed government, however, and rejected the military nominee (General Faruk Gürler) to the presidency of the republic. Nevertheless, by electing the constitutionalist Admiral Fahri Korutürk, parliament agreed in effect that the presidency was the preserve of the military.

The Turkish military had long been used to running their own affairs, free of civilian interference. After 1960, they aspired to, and to some degree achieved partnership in, ruling the state. The process of establishing the supremacy of civil power, which the constitution has always preserved in principle, has been lengthy. At the time of this writing, principle and practice coincide.

In the elections held under the amended constitution on October 14, 1973, the RPP profited from the split in the ranks of the center-right and emerged as the strongest single party. Its leader Bülent Ecevit then redrew the political map by forming a coalition government with the Islamist National Salvation Party, led by Necmettin Erbakan. Ecevit's declaration that the secularist-Islamist split in Turkish society had been a "historic mistake" did not, however, have lasting results.

The most important single decision of the first Ecevit administration was to land Turkish troops in Cyprus in July 1974, after the overthrow of the president of Cyprus Archbishop Makarios III, in a coup organized by the military junta in Athens. The landings led to the occupation of one third of the island by Turkish troops, up to a line that has not shifted to the present day, and to the fall of the junta in Athens.

Responding belatedly to the Turkish military intervention in Cyprus, in February 1975 the U.S. Congress imposed a complete embargo on all arms shipments to Turkey on the grounds that Turkey was improperly using arms supplied for NATO defense. The embargo was relaxed in September of the same year and lifted completely in September 1978 (under the second Ecevit administration), having failed to influence Turkish policy in Cyprus. Turkey had retaliated for the embargo by closing a number of U.S. installations. Limitations on their use were ended when the embargo was lifted. Since then, however, the recurrent renewal of the U.S.-Turkish Defense and Economic Cooperation Agreement (DECA), which regulates the U.S. military presence in Turkey and confers various advantages to Turkey in return (an arrangement that amounts to, but may never be called, a rental agreement), has been the occasion for tough bargaining.

More seriously, the experience of the embargo has led Turkey to extend its own defense industry, earlier confined largely to the manufacture of light arms and ammunition. But the new industry, born of the U.S. congressional embargo, could only be created with the help of U.S. funds and technology. Today, as Turkey manufactures under license F16 fighters, armored personnel carriers, and other kinds of U.S.-designed war materiel, it is clear that the politicians who had argued for the embargo have achieved results that they did not expect.

Bülent Ecevit also upset U.S. opinion by lifting the ban on the cultivation of the opium poppy, which had been imposed by the military-backed administration of Nihat Erim. But the safeguards introduced by the Turkish government seem to have been effective; although drugs are smuggled through Turkey (as they are through other countries), and often by Turkish nationals, locally produced opium is, by and large, used properly for medical purposes.

Almost immediately after he had secured the Turkish zone in northern Cyprus in August 1974, Ecevit tried to put to political use the acclaim that the Cyprus operation had won him at home. Believing that he could force a general election, he dissolved his coalition with Erbakan. But in Turkey it is always difficult to persuade parliament to vote for a dissolution: deputies are determined to reap for as long as possible the advantages they had achieved at dear cost. Rather than agree to an early election, therefore, Erbakan teamed up with Demirel's Justice Party in a series of "Nationalist Front" coalitions, which included also the extreme Nationalist Action Party of Alpaslan Türkeş (a retired officer who had played an active part in the first 1960 coup, but who was removed from the junta, together with 13 other ill-assorted hotheads, a few months later).

Between 1975 and the end of 1977, "Nationalist Front" coalition governments presided over a deteriorating security situation, which was compounded by the economic difficulties arising from the first oil shock in 1973. Demirel's attempt to ensure continued economic growth by increasing foreign borrowing served only to postpone the day of reckoning.

In January 1978, Ecevit, whose RPP had emerged strengthened from the 1977 elections but was still short of an absolute majority, tempted a number of Justice Party deputies to help him form a new government. It proved even less successful than its predecessor. Clashes between leftist and rightist militants developed into a mini-civil war that claimed the lives of prominent figures, such as liberal newspaper editor Abdi Ipekçi, and spread into sectarian violence between the majority Sunnis and the Shi'ite minority in central and eastern Anatolia.

Ecevit's management of the economy was disastrous. His inability to obtain foreign finance during the admittedly difficult conditions following the fall of the shah of Iran led to an acute shortage of foreign exchange and therefore of essential imported goods, including crude oil.

On October 14, 1979, the RPP was decisively defeated in senate elections and lost all five by-elections to the assembly. Faced with this overwhelming proof of its unpopularity, the government resigned. The poor record of the Ecevit administration has been a millstone around the necks of Turkish Social Democrats ever since.

On November 12, 1979, Süleyman Demirel reassumed power at the head of a Justice Party minority government. To describe the time, a phrase has entered Turkish political folklore: the country did not have five cents to its name. In an exceptionally harsh winter, there was not enough fuel for heating. Energy cuts immobilized elevators in the new high-rise buildings in the capital and, more seriously, interfered with the work of hospitals.

On January 24, 1980, the new administration took decisive action to remedy the economy's chaotic state. The traditional goal of containing imports was abandoned in favor of increasing exports by liberalizing trade, devaluing the currency, and gradually abandoning controls over prices and interest rates. As negotiations began to reschedule the foreign debt, fresh foreign finance became available, and consumer goods reappeared in the shops. Although the first effect of the measures was to raise inflation above 100 percent, the rate dropped quickly (from 110 percent in 1980 to 37 percent in 1981, in terms of consumer prices).

The "measures of January 24" had been worked out by Turgut Özal, whose career resembled closely that of

Süleyman Demirel. Like Demirel, Turgut Özal trained as an engineer on a state scholarship and then rose rapidly in the public service, where he won the support of Prime Minister Süleyman Demirel. When Demirel was removed from office in the 1971 "coup by memorandum," Özal found a job with the World Bank in Washington. At about the same time, Atilla Karaosmanoğlu, a Turkish economist employed by the World Bank, traveled in the opposite direction to become a member of the military-backed government of Nihat Erim. Although Karaosmanoğlu resigned from the Turkish cabinet after a few months and resumed his career in the World Bank, Turgut Özal used his experience in the United States to further his career in Turkey. He first entered politics in the ranks of the Islamist National Salvation Party. Unlike Demirel, however, Özal was unsuccessful in his first foray into politics. He then took a management position in the private sector of the economy before being appointed head of the state planning organization when Demirel returned to power at the end of 1979. Özal owed his subsequent career to the success of the "measures of January 24."

Economic restructuring did not help Demirel alleviate social tensions or limit the depredations of terrorism. As the bloodletting continued (claiming among its victims former prime minister Nihat Erim), the future of the government was threatened by the Islamist National Salvation Party, which, irked by its exclusion from the administration, tried to pick off Demirel's ministers in successive votes of no-confidence. On September 5, 1980, Demirel had to sacrifice his foreign minister Hayrettin Erkmen, who had earlier decided to apply for full membership in the EC against the wishes of the Islamists. Parliament was deadlocked by its failure to agree on a successor to president Fahri Korutürk.

The political deadlock was broken by the high command of the armed forces under the chief of the general staff, General Kenan Evren. On September 12, 1980, the military took over power, dissolved parliament and all existing political parties, detained leading politicians, and banned all political activity.

The clampdown that followed was more extensive than in either 1960 or 1971. In four years nearly 180,000 people were detained and nearly 65,000 taken before the courts, which handed down 42,000 sentences, including 326 death sentences.[4] Most of these were commuted, but 25 terrorists— all, it seems, directly involved in killings—were hanged. The main mistake of 1960 was not repeated, however, and leading politicians escaped lightly.

Although the 1960 coup had been popular with the secularist establishment, the coup in 1980 enjoyed much wider support on the part of people who felt personally threatened by the disorder of the previous decade. In the two years before the coup, more than 5,000 people had been killed and 14,000 injured in terrorist incidents. In the first eight months after the military takeover, the number of murders dropped to 230 and injuries to 560.[5] Terrorism was not eliminated, but its scale was reduced dramatically.

The high command, which substituted itself for parliament, appointed retired admiral Bülent Ulusu to head the government. Ulusu retained the services of Turgut Özal, this time as deputy prime minister, and thus saw to consistently implementing the economic liberalization program. This had, of course, become much easier, as labor unions could no longer strike against the drop in real wages.

Inevitably, difficult living conditions gradually eroded the popularity of the military administration. In 1982, Turgut Özal distanced himself from the military by resigning when his tight-money policies led to the collapse of a speculative finance house, to the detriment of thousands of small savers.

Once again, the military formed a consultative assembly to draft a new constitution. Reacting to the politicization of all aspects of life, which was the unintended result of the 1961 constitution, it now sought to restrict political activity to parties represented in parliament. Parties were no longer allowed to have women's and youth branches; politics were banned on campuses, which were purged of anyone accused of radicalism and which were subjected to the central control of a nominated Higher Education Council; trade unions and professional asociations were not allowed to have political affiliations, and radical unions were banned. The leaders of all political parties predating the coup were temporarily banned from politics.

To avoid political fragmentation, a new electoral law required parties to receive at least 10 percent of the nation-wide vote before gaining any seats in parliament. Deputies were not allowed to change parties. As a temporary mea-sure, all founders of new parties had to be approved by the military. The aim of General Kenan Evren and of his military colleagues was to renew the political class and restrict politics to a polite contest between two parties, one of the center-right and one of the center-left, under handpicked, safe leaders.

The new constitution was submitted to a referendum on November 7, 1982, and approved by 91 percent of vot-ers; the support of those who favored the change to more restricted politics was augmented by the votes of people who viewed approval of the constitution as the only means to an early reversion to civilian rule. Under a provisional article, approval of the constitution entailed the election of General Evren for a seven-year term as civilian president of the republic.

Yet the country deviated from the route mapped out by the military. In elections held on November 6, 1983, voters rejected both the party of the center-right, headed by a retired general, and the new party of the center-left, in favor of the only other party that the military allowed to take part in the contest. This was the new Motherland Party, founded by Turgut Özal, according to the old win-ning formula of combining economic and political liberal-ism with cultural conservatism. Describing itself as both nationalist and conservative, the Motherland Party drew support from moderate Islamists and nationalists, but also from liberals in its campaign for a free market economy. A last-minute television appearance by General Evren, which was construed as a warning against voting for the Motherland Party, did not prevent the latter from winning 211 out of the 400 seats in the new single-chamber parliament, or 45 percent of the total poll.

Once his new government was endorsed by parliament on December 26, 1983, Turgut Özal set about extending the trade liberalization measures that he had worked out before the military intervention. The results were impressive. In the first four years of his administration, annual economic growth averaged 6.7 percent. Exports, which had already risen as a result of the measures taken in 1980, increased again from U.S.$5.9 billion in 1983 to more than U.S.$10 billion four years later. Rapid expansion of the tourist industry together with increasing, although still modest, amounts of direct foreign investment, helped restore Turkey's creditworthiness, and the consequent ample availability of foreign exchange allowed the Turkish lira to become a convertible currency. Shops filled with consumer goods, many of foreign origin, and those citizens who could afford it could travel abroad, taking with them as much currency as they liked. Telecommunications, which had been badly neglected, were modernized, and electrification pushed forward. Everywhere there were visible signs of Turkey's growing integration in the global free market. The Istanbul stock exchange was revived and became the arena of speculation.

The number of entrepreneurs increased, but so, it seems, did corruption. The expression "turning the corner" – by fair means or foul – entered everyday vocabulary. Two main methods were used to boost exports; the first was currency devaluation, the second generous financial incentives, disguised as tax repayments. Fraudulent export declarations allowed unscrupulous businessmen to get rich quickly. Insider trading on the stock exchange was another avenue to instant riches. So were kickbacks on public works contracts and public procurement. Questions were raised about the wealth acquired by the families of Prime Minister Turgut Özal and other politicians.

Moreover, economic policy was constrained by political pressures. As the repressive measures introduced by the military were softened, the fall in real wages was reversed. This coincided with the parliamentary elections of November 1987, in which the the Motherland Party's share of the poll fell to 36 percent, while, thanks to divisions in the opposition and a judicious change in the electoral law, its share of parliamentary seats increased to 66 percent. Prime Minister Özal tried to reverse the growing unpopularity of his government by allowing wages to explode and by increasing public spending on farm subsidies, major investment projects, and the public payroll. But the inevitable rise in inflation continued to feed discontent.

In the local government elections held in March 1989, the Motherland Party's share of the poll slumped to 22 percent, and control of the major cities (Istanbul, Ankara, Izmir, and Adana) was won by the opposition Social Democratic Populist Party (SDPP), now led by Professor Erdal Inönü, son of president Ismet Inönü. The SDPP was born of a merger between the Populists (the center-left party formed by the military after 1980) and members of the old Republican People's Party, who had created their own Social Democratic Party. Yet when the ban on the political activity of leading politicians active before 1980 was lifted by a narrow majority in a referendum in September 1987, the old RPP leader Bülent Ecevit stood aloof and founded his own Party of the Democratic Left, thus splitting the center-left constituency.

The center-right was similarly split, as Demirel reemerged to head the new True Path Party (a name better translated as Party of the Right Path), which had been founded on his behalf by the core of his old associates. Demirel found a strong following among farmers, whom the Motherland Party had originally neglected in favor of industrialists and financiers.

In November 1989, when Kenan Evren's presidential term expired, Turgut Özal had himself elected president of the republic by the votes of the parliamentary group of the Motherland Party and left a proxy (Yıldırım Akbulut) in charge of the government. Özal had always taken personal charge of foreign policy, seeing it as the political aspect of his economic policy of integrating Turkey in the world economy. As prime minister in 1987, he had taken the initiative in applying for full membership in the European Community. After his election to the presidency, he similarly took the lead in aligning his policy on that of U.S. President George Bush before and during the Gulf War. In the last months of his life, he devoted his energy to promoting close relations with the Turkic republics of the former Soviet Union, where, he believed, Turkey could spearhead joint Western interests and win appropriate rewards from its Western allies.

Turgut Özal's attachment to the American alliance was strengthened by the end of the cold war and by the collapse of the Soviet bloc, then of the Soviet Union. He believed he had a special personal relationship with President Bush and with Britain's prime minister Margaret Thatcher. But when Özal died on April 17, 1993, neither came to his funeral.

Although Özal persisted in attempts to influence day-to-day government policy, his effective power decreased when Yıldırım Akbulut was replaced in June 1991 as leader of the Motherland Party, and consequently as prime minister, by a younger politician Mesut Yılmaz. Özal's power, although not his interference in government, then ended when the Motherland Party was defeated in the general elections of October 1991.

In these elections, the True Path Party emerged as the single strongest party (with 40 percent of parliamentary seats, won with 27 percent of the poll), and its leader Süleyman Demirel formed a coalition government with Erdal İnönü's Social Democrats (who had won 20 percent of the seats in parliament with 21 percent of the total poll).

Demirel had promised during his campaign to remove Özal from the presidential palace (on the grounds that the parliamentary majority that had elected the president was by that time unrepresentative). He also promised to move swiftly to prosecute Motherland Party politicians guilty of corruption. In fact, a modus vivendi developed between prime minister and president, and Demirel was lavish in his praises of Özal when the latter died on April 17, 1993, and was buried with great pomp outside the walls of Istanbul.

Özal had been incessantly criticized during his terms of office as prime minister and president, particularly by Turkey's intellectual establishment. But when he died, his role in opening up Turkey to the world and in putting Turkey on the world map was widely acknowledged.

Demirel, who had been reluctant to leave the country when he was prime minister in the 1960s and 1970s, emulated Turgut Özal's incessant foreign travels when he returned to office at the end of 1991. At home he was faced with two major problems—ending Kurdish disaffection in the southeast and bringing down inflation. By the time Özal died, Demirel had not made an impression on either problem. Like Özal in 1989, he then opted for the presidential office, to which he was elected by the votes of the parliamentary supporters of the two coalition partners. But this time, neither the legality nor the propriety of the election was contested.

In June 1993, Mme. Tansu Çiller, an American-trained professor of economics who had played a prominent part in Demirel's 1991 electoral campaign and subsequently became minister of state in charge of the economy, was elected to the vacant leadership of the True Path Party. She then became prime minister, heading once again a coalition with the Social Democrats. In September 1993, the deputy prime minister Erdal İnönü left office when he stepped down as leader of the Social Democrats and was replaced by the new party leader Murat Karayalçın, who had made his name as mayor of Ankara.

In March 1994, the Social Democrats lost control of the main cities, which they had governed during the previous five years. In elections to provincial councils, the True Path Party retained the lead, although its share of the total vote dropped to 22 percent, while that of its Social Democrat partners slumped to 14 percent. The Motherland Party received 21 percent of the vote, failing to capitalize on growing discontent. The main beneficiaries were the Islamists of the Welfare Party, whose share of the poll rose to 19 percent and whose candidates were elected mayors of the Istanbul and Ankara metropolitan areas (see chapter 5). The extreme right-wing Nationalist Action Party won 8 percent of the poll, testifying to the shift to the right among the country's voters.

Immediately after Mme. Çiller took office, the aggravation of economic imbalances and of ethnic Kurdish terrorism seemed to threaten President Özal's vision of Turkey as a great regional power, not to mention his prophecy that the twenty-first century would be the "Turkish century." Since 1950, exaggerated optimism has alternated with exaggerated pessimism in evaluations of Turkey's prospects. But through all these mood changes, the country has become stronger in its democratic institutions and more prosperous. Unlike its neighbors, it has avoided wasting its substance either on foreign adventures or on unwise social experiments. As the number of Turks has increased, the lot of the average Turk has improved. At the time of this writing, Turkey's attention is focused more on difficulties and dangers than on achievements. Foreign observers can take a longer view.

2

The Kurds

Kurdish nationalism constitutes the biggest single political problem Turkey faces today. The republic of Turkey, founded as the Turkish national state, was assumed to be nationally homogeneous. Turkish schoolchildren used to be taught the rhyme: "Anadolu, Anadolu, baştan başa Türkle dolu" ("Anatolia, Anatolia, full of Turks from end to end"). The truth is more complicated.

The republic was and remains religiously homogeneous: more than 99 percent of its inhabitants profess the Muslim faith. The founding fathers of the republic equated Muslim with Turk. In this they followed the usage of those Western authors who for centuries spoke of converts to Islam as people who "turned Turk." But inside Turkey, the equation was more recent and was introduced almost imperceptibly.

The National Covenant was adopted by the final Ottoman parliament on February 17, 1920, and then served as a statement of the aims of the nascent republic. It declared that the territory still under Ottoman control when the armistice ended the hostilities of World War I was "an entity, indivisible in fact and in law for whatever reason, composed of those parts [of the empire] which are inhabited by an Ottoman Muslim majority, united in religion, race and origin, imbued with feelings of mutual respect and sacrifice, and governed by customs and social rules which accord fully with local conditions."[6]

There was no mention of Turks, but the assumption that these Ottoman Muslims shared a common racial (today the term is *ethnic*) origin prepared the ground for future policy.

The War of Independence, which preceded the proclamation of the republic, was waged in the name of the Grand National Assembly. Later the adjective *Turkish* was added to the assembly's official title. Today Kurdish nationalists see this as a usurpation by Turkish nationalists of a victory won by both peoples. In fact all local Muslims – not only Turks and Kurds – were involved in the struggle for independence.

The inhabitants of the republic have diverse ethnic origins. Some have lived in Anatolia for centuries: the Turks who first came in the eleventh century, the Kurds who have lived in the mountains of the southeast since the dawn of recorded history and who began embracing Islam in the seventh century, the Arabs in the south, the Laz – a Caucasian people, akin to the Georgians – who live in the northeast and were converted to Islam from the fifteenth century onward. Other Muslims started coming as refugees when the Ottoman Empire began to contract at the end of the seventeenth century and when Russia began to expand south in the eighteenth century. Turkey is thus home to descendants of Balkan Muslims with Bosnian, Albanian, and Turkic origins; of Tatars from the Crimea, the Volga basin, and the Russian steppes; of Circassians, Abkhazians, and other Muslims of the Caucasus. Considerable numbers of Azerbaijanis fled to Turkey after the Bolshevik revolution, while after World War II there were Kyrgyz refugees from Afghanistan and some Uighurs from Chinese Turkestan. The flow of Muslim immigrants has never stopped. The latest to arrive in large numbers were Bulgarian Muslims (of Turkish, Slavic, or mixed origin), expelled in 1989 by Bulgarian Communist dictator Todor Zhivkov.

Mustafa Kemal Atatürk, as Turkey's founder, sought to unite all these Muslims under the banner of Turkish nationalism. His motto—"Happy is he/she who calls himself/herself a Turk" (not "Happy is he/she who is a Turk") — stressed choice and personal commitment over origin. But the accompanying injunction "Citizen, speak Turkish!" had a coercive ring.

In fact none of the constitutive ethnic components of the Turkish citizenry presents a political problem, with the exception of the Kurds. The refugees and their descendants have chosen Turkey and wish to see it one, strong, and undivided. Of indigenous peoples, the Laz see themselves as frontiersmen of Islam and defenders of the Turkish state. The urban Arabs of southern Turkey were good Ottomans under the sultans and are good Turkish citizens today. Only the Nusairi (in Turkish, Alevi) Arabs of the province of Hatay, which was transferred from French-mandated Syria to Turkey in 1939, may in some cases wish to see themselves under Syrian Arab rule. Thus it carries little force to argue that if concessions were made to Kurdish nationalism, Turkish citizens of other ethnic origins might wish to imitate the Kurds and in so doing break up the mosaic of Turkish society and destroy the Turkish state.

The Kurds are a case apart, first and foremost, by reason of their number. Other factors have also contributed to the insistence of a growing number of Kurds in Turkey that their separate national identity should be recognized and provision made for it.

Kurds are concentrated in their original habitat in the southeast, where they form a majority of the population. This majority increased with the departure of the Armenians who had lived among the Kurds for centuries until their uneasy coexistence ended during World War I.

Turkish Kurds also have numerous kinsmen in neighboring countries. The 3.5 million or so Kurds in Iraq and the half million or more Kurds in Syria share the Ottoman past of Turkish Kurds. They were divided from them by the territorial settlement that followed World War I. The 3 to 4 million Kurds in Iran and the 100,000 or so Kurds in Azerbaijan and Armenia were all originally subjects of the Persian shahs and their vassals. But the frontier drawn between the Ottoman and the Persian empires in 1639, which has remained more or less unchanged since then, was porous until recent times, and Kurds on either side have been in contact with each other whenever conditions permitted.

The experience of the Kurds in neighboring states has exercized considerable influence on Turkish Kurds. Iraqi Kurds have enjoyed some measure of official recognition since the days of the British mandate. When they sought more, their struggles inspired their kinsmen in Turkey. Kurdish nationalist feeling in Turkey was similarly affected by the brief existence of the Kurdish republic of Mahabad in Iran, which was formed under Soviet protection in 1946 and dissolved by Iranian troops later in the same year. But it was, above all, the formation of the Kurdish Democratic Party in Iraq and the first campaign fought by its leader Mullah Mustafa Barzani against the central government between 1961 and 1970 that influenced the growth of nationalism among Turkish Kurds. "We are all Barzani's children," declared a Turkish Kurd (Hamit Bozarslan) at a conference on Kurdistan held in London in 1992.

The term "Turkish Kurd," meaning a Kurd who is a Turkish citizen, is perforce imprecise, since the assumption of a national identity is a matter of subjective choice, which is usually based on some objective elements. Current official usage in Turkey prefers the term "people of Kurdish origin." The term "Kurdish-speaker" is also used. But apart from being cumbersomely periphrastic, neither alternative escapes imprecision.

In an ethnically mixed society, where mixed marriages are common, ethnic origin cannot always be determined. Language is the primary basis on which an ethnic identity is chosen. But some Kurdish nationalists speak little Kurdish, and many are more comfortable in Turkish than in Kurdish.

Some Turkish nationalists claim that there is no such thing as a Kurdish language, but only a congeries of rude country dialects. Most linguists disagree. There are in fact two distinct Kurdish languages spoken in Turkey. The majority of Turkish Kurds speak the northern Kurdish language, usually called Kurmanji (Kırmancı in Turkish spelling), although some Kurdish nationalists prefer the term "Badinani" or "Behdinani" (after the former Kurdish principality of Badinan/Behdinan, north of the Great Zab river in northern Iraq). Use of Kurmanji extends into Iraq, as far as the Great Zab, and into Syria; it is also spoken by the Kurds of Transcaucasia.

Although it has a number of dialects, Kurmanji has been more or less standardized and orthographically fixed. It is written in Latin characters by Turkish Kurds and in the Arabic script by Iraqi Kurds. Before the dissolution of the Soviet Union, Transcaucasian Kurds had to use the Cyrillic alphabet to write their language.

The second Kurdish language spoken in Turkey is Dimili. It is known as Zaza in Turkish, after the name of a group of tribes that constitute the majority of the population in the province of Tunceli (formerly Dersim), west of Erzurum. There are also pockets of Zazas, living among Kurmanji-speakers south and east of Tunceli.

Many, if not most, Zazas are Shi'ite (Alevi), while the majority of Kurmanji-speakers are Sunni. Many Zazas, especially outside their home ground of Tunceli, know or at least understand Kurmanji. But, as a rule, Kurmanji-speakers do not understand Zaza. The two languages are not mutually intelligible. Nevertheless, both Zaza-speakers and Kurmanji-speakers consider themselves to be Kurds.

Zaza, like Kurmanji, is written in the Latin alphabet, using Turkish orthographic conventions. Such few publications as have appeared in the language have helped to standardize it.

There are two other Kurdish languages spoken outside Turkey. Iraqi Kurds, living south of the Great Zab, as well as most Iranian Kurds, speak Surani (also known simply

as Kurdi). Surani is usually written in the Arabic script. It
has achieved some preeminence as the language spoken in
Sulaymaniyah, the main Kurdish city in Iraq. Although
Kurdish nationalists consider Kurmanji and Surani to be
two dialects of the same language, they are not readily
mutually intelligible. This limits the impact inside Turkey
of the broadcasts in Surani that are beamed from Sulaymaniyah or Baghdad. Finally, a minority of Iranian Kurds
speak a language called Gurani (or Hawrami), which is akin
to Zaza.[7]

When an attempt was made in 1991–1992 to launch a
national Kurdish newspaper in Istanbul (an attempt that
failed for lack of commercial backing), the language chosen
was Kurmanji, but the specimen edition contained two
pages in Dimili (Zaza). Both Kurmanji-Turkish and Dimili-
Turkish dictionaries are now on sale in Turkey.

The last Turkish census that included linguistic data
was carried out in 1965. At that time, 2,200,000 or 7 percent of the total population of 31,151,000 stated that Kurdish (Kurmanji) was their mother tongue; another 429,000
or 1.4 percent gave Kurdish as their best second language.
The census showed that Zaza was the mother tongue of
150,644 persons and the best second language of another
20,000. Assuming that all those who gave a Kurdish language as their best second language were ethnic Kurds and
treating both Kurmanji and Zaza-speakers as Kurds, one
arrives at an official figure of 2,820,000 ethnic Kurds in
Turkey in 1965 (or 9 percent of the total population).[8]

Yet this figure is likely to have been an underestimate.
Although Turkey was governed by a fairly liberal parliamentary regime in 1965, the use of Kurdish was, at the
very least, discouraged, and many respondents no doubt
found it politic to deny all knowledge of the language. A
more recent estimate gave the total number of Kurds in
Turkey as 7.5 million in 1975, or 19 percent of a population
then amounting to 40.1 million. Of these, 6.5 million were
said to be in the southeast and another million spread
throughout the country.[9]

Since then two tendencies have been at work. First, the gross birth rate is much higher in the east and southeast (37 per thousand), where most ethnic Kurds are concentrated, than in the rest of the country (average of 28 per thousand in 1989). Even when adjusted for higher mortality rates (and particularly the rate of infant mortality, which is 104 per thousand in the east and southeast against a countrywide average of 66 per thousand), these figures mean that the proportion of ethnic Kurds in the population is rising.[10]

In 1992, President Özal shocked Turkish opinion by declaring that there were 12 million Kurds in the country. This rough estimate seems to have been based on the assumption that ethnic Kurds consituted some 20 percent of a population that was approaching 60 million.

The second tendency has been an accelerated movement of people from villages to towns and from the north and east to the west. This movement has been particularly pronounced among ethnic Kurds, because their traditional homeland is comparatively poor and also because many wish to escape the confrontation between security forces and Kurdish ethnic terrorists.

There is broad agreement in Turkey that the Kurdish areas have been economically neglected, while Kurdish nationalists (and many Turkish leftists) claim that they have also been exploited. As a result, Turkish governments have for some years now been discriminating positively in favor of the east and southeast in their investments and economic planning. Yet an analysis of central government receipts and expenditure certainly does not bear out the charge of exploitation. The provinces where most Kurds live receive much more from the central treasury than they contribute to it in taxes. The current policies – swelling the public payroll in the southeast, both for security purposes and to decrease the number of discontented unemployed people, and directing public investment to the region – are only part of the reason.

Contrary to the claims of Kurdish nationalists, the

southeast is poor in natural resources. It produces some crude oil (4.3 million tons in 1992), copper (from the loss-making and overworked mine at Ergani), and other minerals in fairly small quantities. Harsh climatic conditions in this largely mountainous area limit the output of agriculture, which, nevertheless, remains the main activity of local people.

Water is the only resource in which the Kurdish mountains are rich. But the main river, the Euphrates, flows through both Turkish and Kurdish areas. (At least in popular usage, it is in fact the boundary between the two.) The harnessing of the Euphrates, first for power generation and now also for irrigation, has swallowed a large part of the Turkish government's investment budget. After the construction of dams at Keban (1975) and Karakaya (1987), work is progressing on the southeast Anatolia project (known by its Turkish acronym GAP), which is based on utilizing the Atatürk dam (completed in 1992) both for power generation and irrigation. Dual-purpose dams are also being built on the Tigris, further east.

GAP, which aims at the integrated economic development of upper Mesopotamia, is sometimes presented as the Turkish government's answer to Kurdish economic discontent. But just as its financing comes from Turkish central government sources, so too its beneficiaries will be Turks and local Arabs as well as the more numerous Kurds. It should help raise living standards in the southeast, but it will also bind that area closer to the rest of Turkey. The power is being fed to the Turkish national grid, and the outlets for the extra farming produce will lie largely to the west of the Kurdish area, and also abroad.

GAP cannot be expected to absorb the whole, or even a large part, of the population increase of the southeast. Migration to the main Turkish cities will thus continue, and probably increase.

As for other investments encouraged by the government in the southeast, many are likely to prove uneconomic. Like the Italian Mezzogiorno, the Kurdish areas of Turkey will derive little benefit from impermanent "cathedrals in the desert." As it is, money earmarked for investment in the southeast often flows back to the west in response to market pressures.

Istanbul, Ankara, and Izmir already have large communities of Kurdish migrants. So does Adana, the chief city of the rich Çukurova (Cilician) plain, and its port of Mersin. Judging by past experience, the second generation of Kurdish migrants outside the traditional Kurdish areas will lose the Kurdish language.

In addition to poor migrants in search of a better life in softer and more prosperous regions of Turkey, most rich Kurds are sooner or later drawn to the lights of Istanbul. As far as the young are concerned, the current central placement system disperses university students throughout the country. But where they have a choice, students of Kurdish origin prefer the more prestigious universities of Istanbul and Ankara to the academic establishments founded more recently in and around the Kurdish area — in Diyarbakır, Elâzığ, Malatya, and Van.

Abdullah Öcalan (nicknamed Apo), the founder of the violent Kurdistan Workers' Party (in Kurdish, Partiya Karkeren Kurdistan or PKK) learned his Marxism as a university student in Ankara from Turkish teachers. The radicalism of PKK was part of the wave of militancy that swept Turkish universities in the wake of the 1968 student riots in France.

The economic integration of the landlocked and essentially poor Kurdish areas and the cultural assimilation of their people accelerated in line with countrywide developments in the years after World War II. Improvements in communications and telecommunications, education, production, and marketing brought Kurdish and other provincial areas increasingly into the national mainstream. Kurdish nationalism is a reaction to this process. It is seeking to reverse not just the forcible, but also the organic, assimilation of Kurds in Turkish society. As a result, where there was ethnic convergence, there is now a distinct danger of ethnic polarization.

During the Turkish War of Independence (1919–1922), the Grand National Assembly in Ankara gave some consideration to the possibility of Kurdish autonomy.[11] But after the foundation of the republic in 1923, the government adopted a policy that denied the existence of Kurds or of any other non-Turkish Muslim ethnic groups. This policy was part of a process of nation building that was pursued in the context of centralization, westernization, and secularization.

Resistance to this policy was not confined to the Kurds. Thus the rioters in Menemen in western Turkey, who demanded an Islamic government in December 1930, were, it seems, ethnic Turks. But resistance was strongest among the Kurds. Republican centralization threatened the last vestiges of authority the Kurdish tribal leaders enjoyed after more than a century of similar centralizing reforms pursued by the sultans. As a result of these earlier reforms, religious leaders (*shaykhs*, or in Turkish, *şeyh*), had come to replace the petty princes dispossessed by the sultans. The secular reforms of Atatürk meant that these natural leaders of the Kurds were to be swept away in turn. Kurdish nationalism was an added ingredient to discontent stirred up by centralization and secularization.

The first Kurdish political organization was formed in Istanbul after the Young Turks reintroduced constitutional government in 1908. The Treaty of Sèvres, which the victorious Allies failed to impose on Turkey at the end of World War I, provided for a separate Kurdish state should local inhabitants want one. This naturally encouraged the few Kurdish nationalists who continued to work underground after the founding of the Turkish republic.

Kurdish ethnic, religious, social and economic discontents were violently expressed in the revolts of 1925, 1927–1931, 1930–1932, and 1937–1938, but none of these revolts embraced the entire Kurdish population. Although some tribes raised the standard of revolt, others sided with the government. The troubles were all local. Divisions among the Kurds helped the government suppress the uprisings. The mountains of eastern Turkey form an ideal terrain for guerrilla activity, but the central government had the whole area firmly under control by the time World War II broke out.

Turkish government policy relied both on repression and on the cooption of local landowners and other notables into the ruling establishment. Large numbers of Kurds were resettled outside the traditional Kurdish areas. But at the same time many Kurdish notables were recruited by the ruling single party, the Republican People's Party, and ended up as members of parliament in Ankara. There was little or no discrimination against people of Kurdish origin in the civil service, the armed forces, or the professions, provided they were content to call themselves Turks.

When the formation of opposition parties was allowed after World War II, the Kurds, like other Turkish citizens, were able to vote in meaningful elections. All the political parties that contended for power sought and found allies among Kurdish notables in the east and southeast. The party allegiance of these notables rested on individual bargains and was fitful, with blocks of Kurdish votes switching from one party to another whenever a better bargain beckoned.

Turkish law has always insisted that all political parties should be nationwide. It banned regional, ethnic, religious, and, by implication, class parties. Today, although the ban on political activity that seeks to promote religious objectives or establish the domination of a particular social class has been removed from the penal code, it is still written into the constitution and the law on political parties. The ban on ethnic and regional parties remains.

Nevertheless, when the first military coup of May 27, 1960, paradoxically introduced a more liberal constitution, some political parties assumed a specific religious or ethnic coloring. In 1968, an ethnic Kurd, Yusuf Azizoğlu, came to lead the short-lived right-of-center New Turkey Party, and there was speculation that this might become a covert Kurdish party. The New Turkey Party disintegrated, however, and the Kurdish vote continued to be split among the major nationwide parties.

The growth of Marxist influence among Turkish intellectuals also played a role in the recent development of Kurdish nationalism. In Turkey, as in much of the Third World, the most potent manifestation of Marxism was in the form of anti-imperialism. It was directed primarily against "American domination," but Kurdish leftists began to argue that they were themselves the victims of Turkish ethnic domination. Active in the Marxist Turkish Labor Party (TIP) and in other nationwide organizations, these Kurdish leftists also formed their own Eastern Revolutionary Hearths (DDO).

The ideological ferment of the 1960s, briefly stilled by the limited military intervention of 1971, revived and was accompanied by terrorism after the free elections of 1973. Underground Kurdish political parties formed, and there were sporadic attempts to publish in Kurdish.

All Kurdish nationalist activity was severely repressed when the army moved in again on September 12, 1980. The constitution, approved in a referendum in November 1982 as a prelude to the return to parliamentary rule a year later, strengthened the amendments introduced after 1971 to entrench the indivisibility of the Turkish state and nation. But it defined Turkishness in a non-ethnic sense by proclaiming that "everyone bound to the Turkish State through the bond of citizenship is a Turk" (article 66).

Kurdish radicals sought a different dispensation. In 1984, the PKK, which had been formed in 1974 and then acquired a base in the Syrian-controlled Bekaa Valley in eastern Lebanon, launched a campaign of terrorism. The PKK's ideology was explicitly Marxist, anti-imperialist, and secessionist. All three elements are still present, although the first and third are now being played down. PKK leader Abdullah Öcalan declared recently that he would call off his "armed struggle" if his party were allowed to operate legally in Turkey. The Turkish government has resolutely refused, arguing that legal status could not be conferred on terrorists.

After the military coup of September 1980, martial law was imposed on the whole country. It was then gradually lifted, but in the Kurdish areas was replaced by a state of emergency, which parliament renews at four-month intervals. Security operations are coordinated by a regional governor in Diyarbakır. In the 1980s, the government recruited a body of armed village guards, who constitute a paid antiterrorist militia. Often membership both of the militia and of terrorist organizations depends on tribal affiliations. Kurdish nationalists accuse the Turkish government of fomenting a civil war among the Kurds and demand the ending of the state of emergency and the disbanding of the village guards.

By the end of 1992, the PKK terrorist campaign had caused more than 5,000 deaths. More than 2,000 occurred in 1992,[12] when PKK terrorists established themselves in the Kurdish "safe haven" in northern Iraq, using it as a base for incursions into Turkey until they were pushed back from the frontier by a Turkish cross-border operation in October–November 1992. For this purpose the Turkish government achieved a limited understanding with leaders of the Iraqi Kurds—Masud Barzani of the Kurdish Democratic Party (KDP) and Jalal Talabani of the Patriotic Union of Kurdistan (PUK). But it regretted that the two leaders decided in October 1992 to proclaim a Kurdish federated state in Iraq in advance of any democratic expression of popular will in Iraq as a whole.

The proclamation of the federated state had resulted from the creation, by force of Western arms, of a Kurdish safe haven in northern Iraq, which owed its survival to the continued presence of an allied air contingent in the joint

NATO base at Incirlik (near Adana in southern Turkey). These facts made Turkey hesitate before extending the allies permission to stay on in Incirlik.

The Turkish government was faced with a genuine dilemma. Permitting the allies to stay on also allowed the Kurdish federated state to consolidate and become the nucleus of a future independent Kurdistan. Were it to force an allied withdrawal, however, then a renewed Iraqi onslaught on the Kurds might drive the latter to seek refuge in Turkey in their hundreds of thousands. At least 60,000 Iraqi Kurds had fled across the Turkish border in September 1988 in the wake of an Iraqi campaign of repression, which culminated in the destruction of the Kurdish town of Halabja and the gassing of its inhabitants. Thousands of these refugees stayed on in Turkey for several years. In late April 1991, after Saddam Hussein had crushed the Kurdish rising that followed the ejection of the Iraqis from Kuwait, half a million Iraqi Kurds sought once again to cross into Turkey. This time the Turkish government did not allow them in. Instead, it cooperated with the allies in establishing a safe haven in northern Iraq, where the refugees then returned.

While trying to live with de facto Kurdish autonomy in northern Iraq, the Turkish authorities intensified their campaign against PKK terrorism inside Turkey. Western liberals criticized the action, particularly when Turkish troops fired on Kurdish demonstrators on Kurdish (and, more generally, Iranian) New Year's Day (March 21, 1992) and later when troops fired back at terrorist assailants in the provincial chief town of Şırnak, destroying much of the town. There were also persistent reports of death squads hunting down Kurdish radicals. The Turkish authorities responded to the criticism by pointing to the scale of the atrocities committed by the PKK, largely against the local Kurdish population.

In March 1993, PKK leader Öcalan declared a limited unilateral truce, a month later extending it indefinitely. But in May the leader of a local terrorist band ambushed two buses and massacred 32 unarmed soldiers and six civilians. Turkish security forces thereupon launched an all-out offensive against the terrorists. By the end of July 1993, the number of people killed in the PKK campaign since August 15, 1984, had climbed to nearly 7,000 inside Turkey, with another estimated 2,000 killed in military operations across the Iraqi frontier. Casualties included some 2,000 local civilians, many of them Kurds opposed to the PKK.[13]

The situation deteriorated in the closing months of 1993. The death toll for the year increased to some 3,000. The township of Lice, near Diyarbakır, shared the fate suffered by Şırnak the previous year, when regional gendarmerie commander General Bahtiyar Aydın was killed there by a PKK sniper. As the PKK tried to enforce local bans on party political activity, on the distribution of national newspapers, and even on the consumption of spirits and tobacco produced by the Turkish state monopoly, as it pursued its campaign of assassination against schoolteachers and other public servants, normal life in large tracts of the southeast was seriously disrupted. The flight of local people to safer Turkish areas accelerated, businesses closed down, and the government had difficulty finding officials willing to serve in exposed positions.

Terrorism produced an angry backlash among ethnic Turks. After a series of terrorist outrages at the end of October 1993, the governor of the ethnically mixed province of Erzurum took the dangerous step of arming Turkish villagers who felt themselves threatened by Kurds.

President Süleyman Demirel sought to reduce tension by stating repeatedly that the Turkish state was capable of crushing terrorism, while preserving the rule of law and the practice of democracy. But repression of terrorism strains democracy at the best of times. Previous Kurdish risings in Turkey were suppressed without regard to democratic niceties. Today a democratic solution requires the support of the majority not only of ethnic Turks, but also of ethnic Kurds.

Ethnic Turkish opinion is at one in demanding that terrorism should be fought to a finish. There is also wide agreement that the government should use such resources as it has to redress regional disparities in economic well-being. But different answers are given to the question what, if any, political reforms are needed to resolve the Kurdish problem (or the "problem of the southeast," as some Turks prefer to call it).

There is, it is true, a superficial agreement on the need to introduce countrywide democratic reforms to ensure full citizen rights. But these rights are difficult to define. The question of minority rights, as distinct from general citizen rights, is even more controversial. The small residual Greek and Armenian communities in Turkey enjoy legal minority rights under the 1923 Treaty of Lausanne. The Jews decided long ago to renounce protected minority status. No other ethnic or religious community is recognized as a minority in Turkey. But lack of legal status does not dispose of the argument that there are ethnic minorities in Turkey and that, among these, the Kurds seek special recognition.

In December 1991, when he became prime minister once again, Süleyman Demirel declared that he recognized "the Kurdish reality." But he subsequently resisted any political changes likely to accommodate Kurdish national sentiment. To do so, he argued, would be divisive.

Kurds participate in all the political parties in Turkey. But at the time of writing, the radicals are concentrated in the Democracy Party (DEP). It was formed in 1993 when the Constitutional Court closed down the Toiling People's Party (HEP), an offshoot of the Social Democratic Populist Party (SHP). HEP, which had 17 members in the Turkish parliament at the end of 1992 (when it was led by Ahmet Türk, a Kurdish tribal leader from the province of Mardin), claimed to be battling for general democratic rights. According to HEP, it is only when the feelings of the Kurdish people can be freely expressed that a settlement can be negotiated. DEP advances similar arguments. In March

1994, DEP leader Hatip Dicle and five other members of the party were arrested after parliament had voted to lift their immunity. DEP boycotted the local government elections later that month, contributing to the success of the Islamist Welfare Party, which won the mayoralty of Diyarbakır.

Behind the rhetoric, there seems to be a realization that the existing and growing dispersion of the Kurds throughout Turkey and the integration of the Kurdish areas in the Turkish economy preclude a separatist solution. DEP is strongest in provinces bordering Syria and Iraq, while Kurdish areas further north continue to vote predominantly for nationwide center parties. But DEP has supporters also in Istanbul, Ankara, Izmir, and Adana, where there are strong Kurdish communities.

Under the circumstances, the insistence of the DEP leadership on "Turkish-Kurdish fraternity" suggests that what the party has in mind is the creation of a binational Turkish-Kurdish state, which predominantly Kurdish areas in neighboring countries could conceivably join one day. Both DEP and other Kurdish politicians probably think that a federal structure would be appropriate for such a state. But this could be discussed at a future date. At present, full democratic rights should be ensured, including full cultural rights for the Kurds. The immediate choice for Turkey's policymakers does in fact involve the extent of Kurdish cultural rights.

Even before Süleyman Demirel had recognized "the Kurdish reality," President Özal had persuaded parliament to remove from the statute book a law indirectly banning the use of Kurdish. Although the use of the Kurdish language had been discouraged throughout the history of the republic and was at times actively suppressed, not until 1983 did the ruling military regime pass a law banning the use of "all languages which are not the primary official language of any one of the states recognised by the Turkish republic." It was no secret that this cumbersome formulation had been devised to avoid foreign criticism that any specific ban on Kurdish would have provoked. Foreign criticism was not avoided, however, and the ban has now been lifted.

The lifting of this ban on Kurdish led to the appearance of a number of publications in that language, none of which has made much impact. The reason is that the number of people literate in Kurmanji (let alone Dimili/Zaza) is small. Even radical Kurds prefer to disseminate their views in and to read Turkish-language journals. At the time of writing, their main organ is the Turkish-language daily *Özgür Gündem*.

The lifting of the ban on Kurdish publications also brought to the agenda a demand that provision should be made for broadcasts and education in Kurdish. The late President Özal suggested that the special public-service television channel serving the GAP area should carry programs in Kurdish. He also declared that people should be free to argue for any solution to the present problem, including even the secession of Kurdish areas, providing they eschewed violence and did not advocate its use.

At present anyone who threatens by word or deed the indivisibility of the Turkish state and nation can be prosecuted. Moreover, the constitution requires all MPs to swear to uphold "the indivisible integrity of the country and the nation" before they can take their seats. This requirement strained the consciences of Kurdish radicals returned to parliament in the 1991 elections. The term "Turkish nation" can be interpreted in the light of the nonethnic constitutional definition of a Turk. But Kurdish politicians would be happier if the "indivisibility of the nation" were left out of the constitution and of consequential legislation. They realize, of course, that those who wish to work within the Turkish political system would have to respect the integrity of the country.

Many Kurds would argue that a form of autonomy or federal structure would not detract from the integrity of Turkey and might even enhance it. But apart from the fact that ethnic Turkish opinion is overwhelmingly opposed to any notion of Kurdish autonomy, the breakup of federal structures in the Soviet Union and Yugoslavia has taken the wind out of the sails of federalists.

There are other ways, however, in which Kurdish political aspirations could be met within a unitary Turkish state. President Özal referred on one occasion to the election of state governors in the United States and suggested that provincial governors might be elected in Turkey too, rather than being appointed, as at present, by the minister of the interior.

In any case, more power could be given to local government bodies that have existed since the last century. Turkish Kurds, like other Turkish citizens, already have the right to vote not only in parliamentary but also in local government elections. In the 1970s, local government bodies began to form regional associations. It is thus not inconceivable that an association of local councils could be set up to cover the predominantly Kurdish-speaking areas of the southeast. There is already such an association in the area of the southeast Anatolia development project.

In the 1980s, mayors and town councils, which are elected separately, were given wider power and allocated more adequate resources. Provincial councils, formed in Ottoman days in the image of the *conseils généraux* in French *départements* (counties), remain, as in France, subject to the control of the provincial governors (*préfets* in France). But in contrast to their position in France, they have been given little work to do in Turkey. Even if Turkey eschews full-blown federalism or a regime of autonomous regions (on the Spanish model), the further development of existing local government structures could increase Kurdish participation in the political process.

Yet to meet the demands of even moderate Kurdish nationalists would require granting cultural rights to supplement such a strengthening of local government. They want to use Kurdish, at least as a second language, in local government, courts of law, education, and broadcasting, as well as for other public purposes (such as announcements in local airports and railway stations).

Given that autonomy and federalism are not a safe options the republic could choose or reasonably be urged to adopt by its friends, Turkey should consider reforms in three areas that would

- grant full cultural rights to the Kurds
- strengthen local government, including the right of local government bodies to combine territorially
- eliminate all legal obstacles to the formation of nonviolent political parties, including regional and ethnic parties.

The last option is referred to in Turkey as permission to form a Kurdish party. In fact, if the ban on ethnic parties were lifted, it would be reasonable to expect not one, but multiple Kurdish parties to emerge, reflecting the deep divisions within Kurdish society.

Objections can be raised that any such reforms would have to await the complete eradication of ethnic terrorism, because the terrorist menace would inhibit the free expression of Kurdish political preferences within local parties to a much greater extent than within existing countrywide parties, which are better able to resist terrorist intimidation.

Decisions about administrative structure – choosing between the unitary and federal models, for example – and about organizing local government do not come within the scope of any human rights convention to which Turkey is a signatory. But the right to form nonviolent political parties of one's choice, as well as the right to be educated in and publicly use one's native language, can be held to be guaranteed by these conventions. It is true that international law as it applies to minorities is still imprecise and that in some cases Turkey has added reservations when it ratified relevant conventions. But even in the absence of clear legal definitions, there is a consensus in democratic countries that fair provision should be made for minority languages and minority rights.

In these circumstances, Turkish political leaders who wish to enhance their country's place in the civilized world community should take the lead in educating majority Turkish ethnic opinion about the implications of choosing Western democracy as the basis of Turkish political and social life. That most ethnic Turks undoubtedly now oppose any political concessions to the Kurds does not absolve politicians of their duty to lead or at least influence public opinion.

Although politicians remain hesitant, the taboo on the discussion of the Kurdish question has lifted in Turkey. Kurdish nationalist literature, including the writings of PKK leader Öcalan, are available in bookshops. Reforms designed to meet Kurdish aspirations are being freely and hotly debated. Turkey's friends should follow this debate, not hiding their own reactions and feelings but conscious of the dangers inherent in ethnic problems in Turkey as elsewhere.

Not all interest in the Kurdish question is inspired by concern for the Kurds. Turkey has many national adversaries who see in the Kurdish question a means of weakening, if not destroying the Turkish republic. On the other hand, well-wishers should realize that the vast majority of both Turks and Kurds wish to continue living amicably together. DEP protests that Turkish-Kurdish fraternity is its chosen ideal are dictated not just by tactical considerations, but by voter preference.

It can be argued that in the last century reforms urged by the European powers contributed to the weakening and eventual disintegration of the Ottoman Empire. Many Turks are conscious of this and tend to treat all foreign advocacy of reforms as ill intentioned. Without concurring in this judgment, one must nevertheless accept that any policy changes Turkey pursues in dealing with the Kurdish question must be freely willed by the majority of ethnic Turks.

The choice is not between assimilating the Kurds and accommodating Kurdish nationalism. Assimilation is an organic process, which has its own logic and can be expected to continue, irrespective of official Turkish policy. The choice is between forcible assimilation and accommodation. There is inevitably the tendency to believe that a final push (what the French call *l'illusion du dernier quart d'heure*) will solve the problem. Against this it can be argued that force will increase resistance to assimilation.

The Turkish government's choice is complicated by external factors, especially by the presence of Kurds in neighboring countries. Until now Turkish policy has always opposed the creation of any Kurdish national entity outside its borders. This, it believed, would inevitably become a focus for sedition inside Turkey. More recently, however, some Turks have argued that a Turkey that has solved its Kurdish problem and within whose borders the Kurds lead a contented life would become a magnet for foreign Kurds. This raises the possibility, in however distant a future, of redrawing frontiers.

Syria and Iran fear such a possibility, as do Arab nationalists in Iraq. At present these three countries in theory agree with Turkey that frontiers should remain sacrosanct, thus precluding an independent Kurdish state. For a long time, Turkish and Arab nationalists shared a common desire to repress Kurdish nationalism. Turks could build on this common ground because they did not fear Arab nationalism, believing that the Arabs could never match Turkish military power. But the experience of Saddam Hussein's regime demonstrated that an Arab adversary can use oil revenue to buy a massive military arsenal. It has changed the threat perception of at least some Turkish leaders, who see danger now in both Kurdish and Arab nationalism. Turkey therefore has to deal with the Kurdish problem in a way that would not increase the potential threat from a neighboring Arab regime.

This situation is one reason why Süleyman Demirel declared in December 1991 that if Saddam Hussein tried to overwhelm Iraqi Kurds, Turkey would move against him. Another reason is, of course, that collusion in the repression of Iraqi Kurds would strain the loyalty of Turkish Kurds to the breaking point.

Today Kurdish nationalism cannot be willed away. Turkey must achieve an accommodation with it, a process that could well be lengthy and certainly delicate. Predicting where it will lead is impossible. Kurdish nationalism could conceivably end up as a cozy, romantic ethnic feeling in the margins of assimilation, as in the case of Welsh nationalism in Britain. Alternatively, Turkey could remain unitary, but become, in practice if not officially, a binational state, as many Turkish Kurds want. In that case, other Kurds might wish to join it.

One possibility to guard against is exacerbating the conflict between Turkish and Kurdish nationalists, which would increase bloodshed and instability not only inside Turkey, but throughout the region. The Kurds are too dispersed and too divided, and the region they inhabit too poor, to make the emergence of a united, independent Kurdistan a viable or desirable option. Western policy should promote the democratic integration of the Kurds, especially in Turkey, the only democratic Muslim country in the region; in so doing, it would also promote the stability of Turkey as a member of the Western community of nations.

3

Growing Pains in the Economy

When Turkey was founded in 1923, it was a poor agricultural country with almost no industry. Skills and capital were scarce. The republic's founding father, Mustafa Kemal Atatürk, was well aware of the importance of economic development. Without it, the political independence he had won for his country could not survive.

Economic nationalism, which Atatürk espoused, was a reaction to the domination of the Turkish economy by foreigners and by non-Muslim minorities in the last phase of the Ottoman Empire. At first, Atatürk hoped that a Turkish entrepreneurial class would develop rapidly to replace the foreigners. But this proved to be a slow process.

The government's role in the economy went beyond its original nationalist objectives, when Turkey's trade, which was based on the sale of a few farm products (such as tobacco and dried fruits and nuts), collapsed in the wake of the 1929 worldwide economic crisis. As protectionism spread throughout the world, the Turkish state set about creating its own protected domestic industry. But unlike other countries under authoritarian rule, Turkey did not give priority to heavy industry. The aims of the republic were more modest: to improve communications by completing a basic railway network and to produce basic consumer goods — at first little more than cloth, sugar, and cement — that it could not afford to buy abroad. Not until 1939 was the first steel mill built with the help of a British loan. The policy paid off in the years of World War II when new state factories supplied basic necessities in manufactures.

Farming, which provided a livelihood for the mass of the people, was meanwhile more or less left to its own devices. Because it had always been carried on largely by Muslim Turks, there was no reason for nationalist intervention. Farmers were not coerced into new forms of collective organization or taxed oppressively. But the prices at which the state bought their produce tended to be low. Otherwise, the role of the state was limited to creating a few model farms and concentrating on the provision of improved varieties of seed. In the late 1930s and early 1940s, village institutes were established to train rural teachers who would then spread technical and social skills. Producers of cash crops were encouraged to form marketing cooperatives, but received little help.

In the years of World War II, the condition of the farming community deteriorated. There were compulsory deliveries of farm produce to feed the large army standing guard over Turkey's neutrality and compulsory labor for mining and other purposes.

When Marshall Plan aid was extended to Turkey after World War II, the United States and other foreign advisers who surveyed the Turkish economy sought to remedy deficiencies in infrastructure, particularly in rural areas, and to liberalize an economy developed behind high protective walls and dominated by the quasi-monopoly of the public sector in manufacturing. A law passed to encourage private foreign investment had only scant results, as the small and over-regulated Turkish market did not look promising. But the lot of the peasants improved dramatically. A basic network of all-weather roads was built with U.S. technical and financial assistance. A wide-ranging program was implemented for constructing dams and irri-

gation and drainage systems. Farm subsidies were introduced and gradually extended.

All the foreign advisers who have visited Turkey in the
past 40 years have urged economic liberalization. Almost
all the Turkish governments have promised it, but political
and vested economic interests have stood in the way.

The private sector has grown prodigiously, now accounting for about two-thirds of the manufacturing industry. But it owed at least its initial growth to high tariffs
and government procurement and incentives. To this day it
suffers from lack of domestic capital. It had to rely for its
investments first on state banks, then on private banks
and foreign partners. In 1991, the public sector still provided 46 percent of gross fixed investment.

In the meantime, the role of the public sector changed
from economic to political. It was designed to provide
cheap essential goods and services, which it did intermittently, usually inefficiently, when not forced to cover its
costs by raising prices. But over the years the public sector
mainly functioned to provide political patronage. Ruling
parties filled the state economic enterprises (SEEs) with
supporters and adjusted the prices charged to the public
to suit their electoral convenience. According to the OECD
country survey in 1992, "in terms of relative size, the Turkish public enterprise sector is large but not out of the range
found among other OECD member countries. . . . But the
salient characteristic in Turkey is the importance of state-
owned enterprises in manufacturing industry."[14]

In spite of constant talk of privatization, the OECD
found in 1992 that the share of public enterprises in total
value-added declined only marginally from 11.5 percent in
1985 to 10.6 percent in 1990. Staff numbered some 600,000,
or 3.5 percent of total employment – only 0.5 percent down
from the figure in the early 1980s.

In 1993, when the government budget deficit was estimated at Turkish lira (TL) 170 trillion (U.S.$15.5 billion),
the losses of state economic enterprises amounted to TL 48
trillion (U.S.$4.4 billion). The burden of loss-making SEEs

falls not only on the government, but also on private companies using expensive intermediate goods (such as iron, steel, and paper) and services (energy and telecommunications) provided by the public sector.

Like the maintenance of loss-making state enterprises, farm subsidies are determined by political pressures. Again, the cost is borne not only by the state, but by local private manufacturers and the consumer. Thus, high cotton prices paid to farmers deprive Turkish textiles of their competitive edge on the world market.

Determining total farm subsidies is difficult, because they are dispensed through various channels (the Agricultural Bank, purchasing agencies, marketing cooperatives) and in several forms (such as guaranteed prices and fertilizer subsidies). In 1993, the cost to the treasury of farm subsidies was estimated at TL 45 trillion (U.S.$4 billion). Total farm subsidies appear to be below those provided by the European Union, although in some cases (such as wheat) Turkish prices are approaching European levels.

The OECD has described agricultural price support in Turkey as "an expensive and ineffective way of achieving income redistribution."[15] In fact it is the distribution of resources that the state does not possess. The main instrument of redistribution is the consequent inflation.

Growth and inflation have gone hand in hand since the first free elections held in 1950. Inflation is a political problem, because governments have found it convenient to allow the country to live beyond its means. Public deficits are financed by printing money, increasing the domestic debt, and borrowing abroad.

In 1993, consumer prices rose by 71 percent – a level of inflation that had changed little since 1988. The domestic debt was estimated at 29 percent of the gross national product (GNP), and the foreign debt exceeded U.S.$60 billion.

Since 1950, the public management of the Turkish economy has been lax; governments have imposed some discipline only when forced to respond to the pressure of foreign creditors. Nevertheless, significant progress has occurred, not only in the growth of the economy, but also in structural adjustment to the world market.

Steady growth over long periods — with sharp variations from year to year, largely for domestic political reasons — constitutes the successful aspect of Turkey's recent economic history. Between 1981 and 1991, the Turkish economy grew at an average annual rate of 5.1 percent — the highest growth rate in the OECD. Annual growth rose to 5.9 percent in 1992, and then to 7.3 percent in 1993.

According to the Turkish state institute of statistics, in 1993 the country's GNP amounted to U.S.$170 billion or U.S.$2,853 per capita, at current rates of exchange. If one applies the OECD coefficient of 1.86 to allow for lower prices in Turkey, the equivalent figures are U.S.$316 billion for total GNP and U.S.$5,307 per capita in terms of purchasing power parities.

The Turkish market is now large enough to attract foreign investment. Foreign direct investment has increased eightfold since the mid-1980s to about U.S.$1 billion a year.

The aims of Turkish economic policy changed radically in 1980. The goal of economic self-sufficiency (through import substitution) was abandoned in favor of integration in the world free market. Tariff and nontariff barriers to imports were lowered, although some sections of domestic industry (notably the automotive industry, which produced nearly 350,000 automobiles in 1993, and pharmaceuticals) still enjoy high rates of protection (around 40 percent). At the same time, legislation on patents has not met all concerns about the protection of intellectual property rights.

Liberalization has gone much further in the financial realm. The Turkish lira is now convertible; money can be moved freely in and out of the country; residents may hold foreign currency accounts in banks both at home and abroad; and banks are free to set their interest rates (although the authorities try, at times, to influence their decisions).

A vigorous stock exchange has developed in Istanbul, although it remains dominated by treasury paper and public sector issues and is subject to sudden speculative movements. After steep falls occasioned by the Gulf War, the index of the Istanbul Stock Exchange rose fivefold in 1993, then sustained heavy losses in the first quarter of 1994.

A regulatory framework was put in place in 1993 with the aim of reducing the incidence of insider dealing and other forms of fraud. A law was also passed setting up a bullion market. Traditionally, Turkish peasants have kept much of their wealth in the form of gold ornaments worn by their wives, and the authorities are trying to induce them to surrender the gold in exchange for interest-bearing deposit certificates. Turkey handles part of the trade in gold with Middle Eastern countries.

The economic reforms of 1980 were accompanied by a steep devaluation of the Turkish lira, which at first overcompensated for the erosion of its purchasing power by inflation. The undervaluation of the national currency, subsidies, and other incentives led to a rapid rise in export earnings from U.S.$3 billion in 1980 to U.S.$10 billion in 1987. Imports rose more slowly from U.S.$8 billion to U.S.$14 billion. Since then, however, the rise in export earnings has slowed down, while imports have grown more rapidly. Devaluation has not always kept pace with inflation, and export incentives have been scaled down. In 1993, exports amounted to U.S.$15 billion, while imports had climbed to U.S.$29 billion.

The 1980s witnessed the rapid development of a tourist industry. Low prices and new hotels have attracted millions of foreign visitors, with Germans in first place. The rise in tourist earnings was interrupted by the Gulf War and was later threatened by PKK terrorism. The collapse of communist regimes brought some compensation, as East Europeans came in search of cheap consumer goods.

In 1992, Turkey's earnings from tourism approached U.S.$4 billion and since 1989 have exceeded Greece's proceeds from tourism. The Turkish industry is particularly sensitive to fluctuations in demand because it labors under a heavy burden of debt.

The rise in exports and in invisible earnings from tourism and the remittances of Turkish workers in Western Europe (and, to a lesser extent, in the Gulf), combined with inward foreign investment, has allowed Turkey to service its foreign debt and continue borrowing. Yet, the International Monetary Fund and other foreign and international agencies have warned repeatedly that the external economic balance was fragile in the face of continuing deficit financing at home. In 1993, Turkey was still able to raise money by issuing bonds on international markets. But in 1994, the country's creditworthiness was downgraded, and the government promised effective action to balance its books.

There was little argument about the means that had to be employed. Clearly, rises in the public service payroll and in farm subsidies had to be restrained, while revenue had to be increased through privatization and better collection of taxes. In 1990, tax receipts in Turkey amounted to 27.8 percent of gross domestic product (GDP) – the lowest proportion in the OECD (the EC average was 40.8 percent). However, neither the Motherland Party governments (1983 to 1991) nor the first coalition government that succeeded it (1991 to 1993) had the will to take the necessary unpopular measures. The challenge was inherited by the second coalition government formed by Professor Tansu Çiller in June 1993.

All Turkish governments since World War II have pursued policies of rapid economic growth through thick and thin. As difficulties arose, they tried to overcome them by ad hoc measures, which have led to constant chopping and changing in economic management. In addition, ministers and to a lesser extent senior civil servants wish to leave a memorial in the shape of monumental public works, such as dams, roads, bridges (currently termed "mega-projects"). To finance them, as well as current expenditures, they borrow at home and abroad, convinced that debts will go away, but physical achievements will survive.

The tendency to borrow abroad, indulged to the full by the last sultans, which led to foreign control over the Ottoman public debt, was countered by the founding fathers of the republic. But it revived as a constant feature of Turkish economic policy after World War II, when U.S. and then other Western aid and credits became available in recognition of Turkey's strategic role in the Western alliance. When Professor Tansu Çiller was selected prime minister in June 1993, she promised to search out every possible source of finance.

Although Greece has developed a culture of dependency on the EC, Turkey was deprived of access to EC funds (largely because of the Greek veto). It has had to rely increasingly on commercial borrowing, which, it is true, is a healthier alternative because sooner or later it imposes some form of economic discipline. The time for this discipline has now come.

What Turkey needs now above all else is a stable, as well as sensible, public policy framework. If it can be set in place, the economy will be able to fully use its many advantages. Unlike the oil-rich Arab states, Turkey has developed on a broad front with a useful specialization in manufactured consumer goods. The Turkish textile industry has been particularly successful in foreign markets and accounts for a large part of export earnings. Its costs have risen, however, and it is now threatened by cheaper producers in South Asia. The burden of heavy industry (such as iron and steel) and of uneconomic activities (such as coal mining) is comparatively small. Turkey is the only country in the region with adequate water supplies. Its ability to feed a population that has increased fivefold since the proclamation of the republic is a major achievement. After satisfying internal needs, Turkey exported farm products worth U.S.$2.4 billion in 1993, against imports of farm products of only U.S.$1.7 billion.

Popular culture is achievement oriented, and a widespread work ethic motivates secular and religious-minded citizens alike. The large family corporations that dominate Turkish industry have achieved internationally accepted levels of efficiency and have shown that good industrial organization can be implanted in Turkey. This modern sector, represented by the Association of Turkish Businessmen and Industrialists (TÜSIAD), coexists with a larger and more traditional commercial community (which dominates the Turkish Union of Chambers of Commerce and Commodity Exchanges) and with the politicized public sector.

In 1991, out of a population of 57.7 million, 33 million fell in the 15 to 64 age bracket and were theoretically available for employment. The actual labor force was estimated at 19.4 million and employment at 17.7 million, of whom 48 percent were engaged in agriculture (which produced only 16.5 percent of GDP). Unemployment was estimated at 8 percent and underemployment at another 6.5 percent, although the prevalence of peasant households affects the accuracy of these figures. Certainly in popular perception, unemployment is a major, if not the major, problem, particularly in less developed areas.

An international survey published in 1992 suggested that in availability of skilled labor and qualified engineers, and in worker motivation and receptiveness to learning, Turkey was in line with OECD standards. Educational attainment was lower, however. Although five-year primary education is universal, only 26 percent of the relevant age group was receiving full-time secondary education in 1988. For tertiary (university) education, the figure was 12 percent. Just as these were the lowest levels in the OECD, so too Turkey was at the bottom of the OECD league in spending only 1.9 percent of its GDP on public education.[16]

In recent years, expenditure on education, both public and private, has increased rapidly, but the rate of youth unemployment remains high. In October 1992, one-third of urban youths were unemployed between the ages of 15 and 24, one-fifth between the ages of 25 and 30.[17]

These figures can be taken as an index of both underdevelopment and the potential for development. The Turkish economy grew at an annual rate of about 6 percent between 1930 and 1939 and, after the interruption of World War II, between 1950 and 1980. Similar growth rates can be sustained now, provided public finances are put in better order and economic management is improved and stabilized. The problem is political, rather than economic.

prob w/ eco dev

4

The Social Scene

Demographics are the main force for change in Turkey. The population of the republic, which numbered 13.6 million at the time of the first census in 1927, rose to 56.5 million at the time of the last census in 1990. Although population growth is slowing down, between 1985 and 1990 the net annual growth rate was still 21.7 per thousand. Population density – that is, the number of persons per square kilometer – rose from 18 in 1927 to 73 in 1990. The Turkish state institute of statistics estimated the country's population in 1993 at nearly 60 million and expected it to rise to 70 million by the year 2000.

Geography dictates the regional distribution of the population. In 1990, nearly a third of all Turks lived in the west – in Thrace and along the shores of the Sea of Marmara and the Aegean Sea, and another 14 percent along the southern Mediterranean coast. Over the last 40 years, the proportion of the population living in the climatically "soft" parts of the country – near the western and southern coasts – has risen from 38 to 47 percent of the total.

In 1990, 23 percent of the total population lived on the central Anatolian plateau – a figure boosted by the location there of the capital, Ankara, and important regional centers (Eskişehir, Konya, and Kayseri). The Black Sea and its hinterland, where the coastal plain is narrow, was home to 11 percent of the total population. The east and southeast (where the majority of Kurdish-speakers is concentrated) accounted for 20 percent. Currently, the Black Sea coast and eastern Turkey are losing population, while in the southeast, emigration is more than offset by an above-average birth rate.

In 1927, 76 percent of all Turks lived in villages, 24 percent in cities and towns. By 1990, the proportion of urban dwellers had risen to 53 percent, while that of the rural population had dropped to 47 percent. Urban population was increasing at an annual rate of 43 per thousand, while rural population was actually dropping at a rate of 5.6 per thousand a year.

In 1990, there were 73 cities with more than 100,000 inhabitants. Their total population, amounting to nearly 21 million, included 6.6 million within the municipal boundaries of greater Istanbul, 2.8 million within those of Ankara, 1.8 million in Izmir, 916,000 in the southern city of Adana (near the main NATO base at Incirlik), 835,000 in Bursa (which draws many Muslim immigrants from the Balkans), and 603,000 in Gaziantep, an ethnically Turkish city whose fortunes are likely to benefit from the southeast Anatolia hydroelectric and irrigation project. Also in 1990, Diyarbakır, the chief city in the Kurdish-speaking area and the seat of the regional governor, had a population of some 380,000. But recently it has been swollen by tens, if not hundreds, of thousands of people fleeing from terrorism and antiterrorist operations.

The population of the province of Istanbul, which is almost totally urban, but does not contain the whole of the conurbation, is expected to rise to 11.2 million by the year 2000, when it will roughly equal that of Greece. By the year 2010, statisticians expect 17 million people will live in Istanbul province, 4.6 million each in Ankara and Izmir provinces, 2.9 million in Adana province (with another 2.7 million in the adjacent Mersin province, which provides its outlet to the Mediterranean), and 3.2 million in Bursa province. The population of Diyarbakır province was expected to climb to 2 million by the year 2010. It will probably reach that level much sooner.

It is hard to provide for the basic needs of this fast-growing urban population. In Istanbul and Ankara, in particular, public transport is inadequate and traffic jams common. Schools teach in two, and sometimes three, shifts. Public hospitals cannot cope with demand. Nevertheless, considerable advances have been or are being made in the main cities: piped natural gas is now available in Ankara, Istanbul, and Bursa; rapid transit systems are under construction in Ankara and Istanbul; the capacity of the water supply and sewerage systems is being increased in Istanbul.

Not only city dwellers but also most villagers are now within reach of road, water, electricity, and telecommunications networks. The number of telephone lines increased from 2.5 per hundred inhabitants in 1980 to 16 per hundred in 1992.[18] Automatic long-distance dialing is available almost everywhere. Modern business aids such as computers, fax, and telex are widely used.

Since the 1950s, the rapid growth of cities has caused shantytowns to mushroom. To what extent is difficult to estimate because they tend to be upgraded over time. Shantytowns around the chief cities are usually connected to water and electricity mains, although not always to the sewerage main. For electoral reasons, squatters are sooner or later issued title deeds. Attempts at razing illegal buildings are fitful and largely ineffective. Small blocks of apartment houses gradually appear among one-story shanties.

The urban shanty, known as a *gecekondu*, is, in any case, often an improvement on the traditional adobe village house of central Anatolia. (*Gecekondu* literally means "put up by night"; convention had it that a building with a roof could not be demolished, and every effort was therefore made to put a roof on in the first night of construction.) From shanties, rural immigrants hope to move to apartments in large apartment blocks. This type of construction, which is beginning to surround all Turkish cities, has been encouraged by the Collective Housing Fund, created in the early 1980s and financed by levies on imports and departure taxes paid by Turks traveling abroad.

The lower-middle and middle classes often become homeowners with the help of housing cooperatives, usually formed on an occupational basis (for officers, doctors, journalists, et cetera). More recently, large construction companies have begun to engage in speculative development, with both public and private banks providing mortgages for the sale of apartments.

The discomfort of life in crowded cities and the pollution of the beaches and countryside in their immediate environment have led the middle classes to acquire summer houses further away: along the coast of the Aegean and Mediterranean seas and more recently the cooler Black Sea. Built also both by cooperatives and by speculative builders, these summer houses have become a distinguishing mark of middle class life in Turkey.

Environmental protection leaves much to be desired. In spite of recent clean-up campaigns, the Golden Horn in Istanbul and the Gulf of Izmir are little better than open sewers. Cities suffer from an acute shortage of open public spaces, parks, playing fields, gardens, and trees. There is no shortage of ambitious urban plans, but these are violated routinely, both by rich and poor. Millions of Turks live in messy concrete jungles.

Nevertheless, the main cities have become cleaner of late. Ankara no longer figures in the list of the 13 Turkish cities with the most polluted air. Istanbul has fared worse, ranking sixth in the list of cities with the highest concentration of sulfur dioxide in the air, and thirteenth in the table of smoke content in the air. The most polluted air is now to be found in provincial cities, like Erzurum, Diyarbakır, and Sivas, which rely on low-grade domestic coal for their heating and industrial power.[19]

The rapid growth of the population has resulted from improved health services and of course the preservation of peace during the republic's 70 years. True, Turkey ranks at the bottom of the OECD league in health expenditures. It spent only 4 percent of GDP, or U.S.$142 per person, in 1991 (calculated in purchasing power parities) and has only 0.9 doctors and 2.4 beds per thousand of population. Nevertheless, between 1960 and 1991, infant mortality dropped from 200 to 66 per thousand, and life expectancy at birth rose from 50 to 68 years for women and from 46 to 64 years for men. Life expectancy at age 60 (18 years for women and 16 for men) is approaching the level of developed countries.[20]

In spite of the increasing numbers of elderly people, the age pyramid in Turkey continues to have a very broad base. The average age of the population in 1985 was 25.5 years, and the ratio of dependency (the number of people aged 0 to 14 years and above 65 years, divided by the number aged 15 to 64 years) was 72 percent. If one takes the Western view of full-time education as extending not between the ages of 7 and 12 years (when it is compulsory in Turkey), but optimally between the ages of 5 and 22 years, then the proportion of Turkey's population within this age bracket in 1985 (the last census for which a breakdown by age is available) amounted to 42 percent of the total.

Although educational qualifications vary (see chapter 3 on the economy), the literacy rate has risen dramatically—from only 19 percent in 1935 to 77 percent in 1985, when 86 percent of all men and 68 percent of all women were classed as literate.

Education is the key to social advancement. Both presidents Turgut Özal and Süleyman Demirel came from humble provincial backgrounds. Both were educated in free state schools and universities and then rose rapidly in the public service (which they had to enter to repay their free education) before entering politics.

Competition for places in the better state schools and universities, as well as in the growing number of private educational establishments, is intense. Ambitious parents put great pressure on their children to achieve, and they spend a large part of their income to place their children on the right educational ladder. At first, most private schools were foreign owned and run. Now there are many Turkish private schools, some of which teach in English. English is used similarly in some public and private universities. Private language schools and tutorial colleges are also proliferating.

Most private wealth has been recently acquired by self-made enterpreneurs or those who benefit from proximity to political power — or a combination of both. The main business dynasties go back to the early years of the republic, when their founders filled the void left by departing foreigners and other non-Muslims. Vehbi Koç (the founder of Koç Holding, the country's largest business conglomerate) was a provincial shopkeeper, who was lucky to be a native of Ankara, the future capital. Sakıp Sabancı (the founder of Sabancı Holding) was a village boy who started by shifting bales of cotton and then acquired a cotton gin owned earlier by a non-Muslim.[21] Eczacıbası Holding was started by a neighborhood pharmacist, who was said to have been the only Muslim pharmacist in Izmir.

The process is continuing. Cavit Çağlar, who helped payroll Demirel's electoral campaign in 1991, was a poor refugee from the Balkans who started at the bottom rung of the rag trade in Istanbul.

As the republican establishment matures, however, the importance of inherited wealth is increasing. Professor Tansu Çiller, Turkey's first woman prime minister, is the daughter of a senior public servant (a provincial governor), whose parents could afford to give her an American education in Istanbul and the United States. Even earlier, left-of-center leader Bülent Ecevit could have a privileged upbringing (at Robert College, an American missionary foundation in Istanbul, which has now become Bosporus University), because his father belonged to the first generation of nationalist politicians.

Landowners played some part in the history of the

republic, but they were rarely very rich, as land produced little revenue. In any case, except in the southeast where some tribal lands were registered in the names of traditional tribal leaders, Turkish agriculture is dominated by smallholdings. In 1991, some 70 percent of all farms, accounting for nearly 60 percent of all cultivated land, covered between 20 and 200 decares (roughly 5 to 50 acres). A third of all farms covered between 20 and 50 decares (5 to 7.5 acres) of land.

In 1987, farming accounted for 23 percent of all household incomes, salaries and wages 24 percent, trade 13 percent, and revenue from real estate 12 percent. Also in 1987, the poorest 20 percent of households, with an average annual income of TL 964,000 (worth at the time about U.S.$1,100) accounted for 5 percent of total household income. The top 20 percent, with an average income of TL 9,190,000 (equivalent to U.S. $10,750), disposed of almost exactly half of total household income. Contrary to a widespread impression, based on anecdotal evidence, the Turkish state institute of statistics estimates that the share of the top 20 percent is dropping and that income distribution is becoming more equitable.[22]

Yet the tendency of the newly rich to indulge in conspicuous consumption reinforces the belief that social inequality and injustice are both widespread and increasing as a result of the official sponsorship of free-market policies. The lavish weddings, luxury villas, yachts, and automobiles of successful entrepreneurs are regularly featured in the popular press, causing resentment among readers, most of whom lead modest, straitened lives.

In fact, the pervading ethos of Turkish life is by now petty bourgeois. Most dream about, and many obtain, a little apartment, a small automobile, basic consumer durables (TV and VCR, stereo, washing machine, sewing machine), adequate schooling, and a fortnight's holiday by the sea. There is much advertising of national brands and no shortage of reasonably priced consumer goods.

The media, as elsewhere, have a pervasive influence. In

mid-1993, viewers had a choice of up to 12 TV channels, of which 4 were run by the government, while all carried advertisements. The legalization of dozens of private radio stations, which had sprung up in defiance of the theoretical ban on private broadcasting, vied with inflation and Kurdish terrorism as the most important subject of public interest.

The total circulation of national newspapers, which had stagnated for some time between 2 and 3 million, rose rapidly in 1992–1993 as a result of aggressive promotion campaigns, most of which relied significantly on gifts of encyclopedias and self-improvement books. In July 1993, three national newspapers, all of a broadly liberal-nationalist tendency (*Milliyet, Sabah,* and *Hürriyet*), had daily sales approaching 1 million copies each. Next in sales were two newspapers of a religious-nationalist hue, *Türkiye* and *Zaman*.

The national press is based in Istanbul, but has editorial offices and printing facilities in several other cities. There are no provincial papers of note, except in Izmir (where the local paper *Yeni Asır* is part of the national *Sabah* group). National newspapers are involved in commercial broadcasting and in magazine and book publishing; they also operate marketing and travel companies, as well as other commercial enterprises.

Although the press has developed rapidly and is technically well-equipped, the country still lacks a serious newspaper of record. Because the press is free and libel laws are lax, sensationalism is frequent. News is of course usually bad news. Flag-waving, self-deprecation, and distrust of foreigners are common themes. "We're poor innocents, and foreigners are always conning us – they're afraid of a strong Turkey" conveys the tone of many nationally famous columnists. Everything that happens at home or abroad is grist for the domestic political mill. The growing financial press, however, is more sophisticated.

Literary and cultural life, although lively, is experiencing the inroads of mass media. There are many theaters,

both state-supported and private, opera and ballet perfor-
mances, art galleries, and, of course, cinemas. The domestic film industry now works mainly for television, although
continuing to produce feature films, whose technical qual-
ity has been improving. Music – Western pop and classical,
Turkish classical, and the so-called arabesque (oriental pop,
which is despised by the elite) – is part of everyday life.

Western and international influences are pervasive.
The arts, like the serious media, are left-leaning, as in
many Western countries. Secularism is politically correct.
So is "anti-imperialism." Feminism and environmentalism
are beginning to make an impact.

Nevertheless, society is still by and large informed by
traditional values. Standards of right (*sevap* – a meritori-
ous act) and wrong (*günah* – a sin) and honor (*namus*) remain strong. Hospitality is prized. Society is held together
by a network of personal connections that confer rights
and impose duties.

The emancipation of women, proclaimed by edict as
part of Atatürk's reforms, has gone a fair way, even though
women remain badly underrepresented in parliament and
generally in politics. Mme. Çiller as prime minister is still
cause for wonder, and so far only one woman has become a
provincial governor. Yet many women hold positions of
authority and eminence in the professions, the judiciary,
private business, cultural affairs, and, of course, educational and health services. Used to the schoolmarm
(*hoca'nım*) from primary school, Turks combine a macho
culture with acceptance of women in authority. In the
home, the mother and elder sister (*abla, bacı*) share authority with the father and elder brother (*ağabey*). Traditional
culture imposes respect for elders.

Following the abandonment of the Islamic *shari'a* code,
Turkish law gives equal treatment to men and women. Nevertheless, gender equality is still confined in practice to the
middle classes. Inequality derives not only from the survival of Islamic traditions, but from traditional regional
Mediterranean culture and nineteenth-century European

models. Thus the legal privileges of husbands derive not from Islam, but from old French definitions of the legal rights of the *chef de famille*.

Although family units living in small apartments inevitably tend to be nuclear families, loyalty to the extended family remains the strongest social bond. People also experience solidarity through their ties to neighborhood as well as village, town, and region; through their shared educational and professional backgrounds; and through their memberships in religious confessions and groups.

Society is permeated by networks of primordial loyalty, affinity, friendship, and material interest. As ideology has declined, political parties have become largely networks of mutual interest and protection. Their role as a force with which to challenge authoritarian public servants has been diminished by the politicization of the administration. But the variety and multiplicity of social and personal pressures has produced not so much democratic order as democratic disorder. Seventy years after the proclamation of the republic, and more than 40 years after the first genuinely free parliamentary elections, Turkey has yet to combine democratic government with effective administration.

The question of human rights in Turkey, which is often raised in the West, is best examined in a social, rather than political, framework. Turkey has signed all the main conventions drawn up by the United Nations and the Council of Europe for the protection of human rights. It has accepted the Paris Charter of the CSCE. It has reformed its domestic legislation to guarantee access to lawyers and limit to a minimum the detention of suspects before they are charged. Torture has been outlawed. When domestic procedures have been exhausted, aggrieved Turkish citizens have the right of individual appeal to the tribunal of human rights in Strasbourg.

This does not mean that abuses of human rights no longer occur. The intensified ethnic terrorism of recent years and persisting ideological terrorism tempt security forces and other organs of the state to take the law into their own hands. As safeguards are built into laws relating to the prosecution of offenders, so too servants of the state, convinced of the guilt of suspects, do on occasion mete out rough justice – shooting to kill or extracting confessions by force. The lives of law-enforcement agents are threatened daily. This influences their behavior.

Moreover, by Western standards, Turkey is still a poor country. Although conditions in prisons have much improved, they fall short of those prevailing in more affluent societies. Poverty can breed abuses, such as bribery, that affect law enforcement and the administration of justice.

Again, there is a tradition of firm, not to mention brutal, law enforcement in a society where many men go about armed with handguns or knives, where disputes, first land and then commercial, have frequently ended in bloodshed as have perceived violations of individual or family honor.

In the past, violence was successfully circumscribed by traditional social networks, family values, and, in the last resort, fear of law enforcement officers. Thanks to these traditional forces, an exploding conurbation like Istanbul remains to this day safer than many Western cities. But traditional society is eroding in Turkey. Aside from terrorism, the incidence of crime is perceived to be rising, seemingly in step with the advance of Western democracy. Consequently, not only the policeman but many a solid citizen has an ambivalent attitude to the new safeguards for human rights. The late president Özal is said to have remarked, "What's wrong with violating the constitution, just for once?" His successor Süleyman Demirel said, in another context, "You mustn't be angry with the state."

Social change, of which democracy's advent is a facet, has undoubtedly brought problems, but it has also brought new safeguards. Courts are by and large independent; so is the press. Parliament is freely elected and functions freely. The institutions of civil society – political parties, labor unions, professional organizations – are growing in strength and can help redress grievances.

Turkish society is remarkably open. Foreigners can come to observe and criticize and then return for the same purpose. Although there are of course cover-ups, means also exist to expose them.

It can be said with certainty that, first, the legal protection of human rights is stronger in Turkey today than ever before, and, second, that it is more effective than in most countries to the north, east, or south of it. One could add that the more open a society is, the more attention its shortcomings receive. Nor is criticism of real or alleged shortcomings always free of ulterior motives. Those members of the European Parliament in Strasbourg (and, in particular, members from Greece) who are loudest in condemning Turkey's human rights record are precisely those who are opposed to Turkey for reasons unrelated to human rights. Again, care is needed that criticism of the human rights record of regimes friendly to the West does not undermine these regimes and put in their place more brutal successors. Bad as the shah's regime in Iran was, Khomeini's proved to be worse.

All this may fail to satisfy critics, including many Turks, who want human rights to be protected in Turkey as effectively as they are in Western societies. No doubt they will be so protected when Turkey's society becomes fully Western in material as well as social aspects. Meanwhile, the Western alliance, which accepted Turkey's membership in the days of the cold war, need have no qualms about welcoming it today.

5

The Religion of Turkey

Turkey is a secular republic, almost all of whose inhabitants are Muslim. On the one hand, the secular nature of the Turkish state sets it apart from almost all other countries with Muslim majorities. On the other hand, Turkey's Islamic religion sets it apart from Western and other rich countries, whose cultures have primarily been molded by different religious traditions but to whose ranks Turkey aspires. In both cases, Turkey's unique mixture of secularism and Islam provide a rich source for misunderstanding.

Westerners worried by the resurgence of militant Islamic fundamentalism wonder whether the secular Turks can resist it. For their part, Turks, including even nominal Muslims who themselves feel menaced by fundamentalism, feel vulnerable to historically conditioned, Western prejudices against Islam.

Most non-Turkish Muslims and a fundamentalist minority in Turkey believe that secularism and Islam are logically incompatible because the latter prescribes rules not only of personal conduct but also of collective governance. How can Turkish Muslims, they ask, allow their state to disregard Muslim law on marriage, inheritance, commercial transactions, the administration of justice, and other secular matters, not to mention the enforcement of religious obligations on the part of individuals? Given that Muslim law is firmly rooted in the Qur'an, which Turkish Muslims accept as divine revelation, logic provides no answer to the question. History does.

Turkish Islam is old: the Turks were already Muslims in the eleventh century when they began the conquest of the territory now held by the Turkish republic. The roots of Turkish secularism are similarly ancient. True, Islam ceased to be Turkey's official religion only in 1928. But, secular considerations (*ruison d'état*) have long taken precedence over religious imperatives in Turkey. Islam was a source of identity, legitimation, personal inspiration, and social mobilization; it influenced, where it did not mold, the Turkish way of life. But from the time of the first sultans, civil ordinances (*kanun*) supplemented, circumscribed, and in practice often replaced the holy law of Islam (*shari'a*).

Islam, Muslim scholars assert, is both a religion and a polity (*al-Islam din wa dawla*). The first Ottoman constitution of 1876 declared that "the Islamic Caliphate [i.e., the succession to the Prophet] is vested in the Ottoman Sultanate" (article 3) and "as the Caliph, the Sultan is the protector of the religion of Islam" (article 4).[23] In fact, contrary to the views of canon lawyers, Islam was the servant of civil power, not the other way around. This is the essence of the "Turkish-Islamic synthesis," which conservative Turkish intellectuals advocate today. Civil power controlled the religious establishment. Rulers took decisions on practical grounds. They then obtained religious endorsement for them from the canon lawyers, whom they employed for the purpose.

Moreover, Islam was never the sole source of either the Turkish way of life or of government practice. Certainly by the end of the nineteenth century, the Ottoman establishment found in France a much more potent source of inspiration. But throughout the history of the empire, both Christian subjects within and Christian powers outside the state exerted a strong influence on the Turks.

What Mustafa Kemal (Atatürk) did in 1928 was to

dispense with Islam as a source of legitimation, abolish the last traces of its influence in civil and personal law, prune its institutions, and starve it of funds. He did not, however, relinguish control over the religious establishment.

State control over religion always had its opponents in the Islamic community. From the earliest times, popular Islam had found a vehicle in religious (dervish) brotherhoods, which had more autonomy than official Islam. On occasion, enthusiasts, particularly among students in religious schools, caused, or contributed to, uprisings against the civil authority, demanding the integral application of *shari'a* law. The last major rebellion under the banner of the *shari'a* occurred in 1909 and was directed against the Young Turks who had seized power the previous year. The uprising was suppressed by the army and its leaders were hanged. Islamic fundamentalism, to use a Western term (the Turks prefer to call it *şeriatçılık* – that is, advocacy of the *shari'a*), has a long history in Turkey. The Turkish state has a similarly long tradition of suppressing it.

Atatürk, of course, went much further than the sultans in his secularist reforms. These reforms are deemed an irrevocable part of the Turkish constitution. But their application has become much more flexible.

Two contrary tendencies are at work in Turkey today. The first is the gradual, organic secularization of society in response to secular education, the growth of consumer culture, the influence of the media, particularly television (which draws many of its programs and all its inspiration from the West), and contacts with the outside world. The opposing tendency is a return to the late Ottoman practice of using religion for purposes of social control and legitimation. There is also a limited, but real, revival of Islamic sentiment as a source of comfort in a difficult world. "I feel comforted when I hear the call to prayer," said Prime Minister Çiller as she assumed power in June 1993. The statement was not necessarily made to attract the religious vote, as her opponents argued.

Turkey has today an unofficial established religion.

Just as the sultan used to appoint the Şeyhülislam (Shaykh al-Islam) as the head of the religious establishment, so now the prime minister appoints the president of religious affairs. In 1994, the presidency of religious affairs was voted an annual budget of TL 8.4 trillion (approximately U.S.$262 million), or just over 1 percent of the total central government budget. It employed 81,000 staff, mainly prayer leaders and preachers, "to enlighten the citizens on the need to protect the integrity of the country and ensure national unity and concord."[24] Most of them are employed in the 70,000 mosques that serve the faithful, subject to state supervision. Most sermons are written or vetted by appropriate officials of the religious civil service.

Although the law on the unification of education remains on the statute book, there were in 1990 some 210,000 students in religious middle schools (for students 12 to 15 years of age), 100,000 in religious high schools (for students 16 to 18 years old),[25] and several thousand in university faculties of theology. All these establishments, as well as the 4,500 or so simpler Qur'anic courses, are funded by the state.

Under article 24 of the constitution, "Education and instruction in religion and ethics shall be conducted under state supervision and control. Instruction in religious culture and moral education shall be compulsory in the curricula of primary and secondary schools." The textbooks, which are licensed by the presidency of religious affairs, teach the principles of Sunni Islam, with a special stress on social responsibility, but always "in accordance with the principles of secularism" (article 136 of the constitution).

Although religious brotherhoods remain formally banned, they are tolerated so long as they do not make a nuisance of themselves. They span a wide range of beliefs and practices—some strictly orthodox, others heterodox, some are activist, others quietist. At least two brotherhoods exercise considerable political influence. The first is the strictly orthodox Nakşibendi (Naqshibandiyya) brotherhood, which has personal (rather than organic links) with the Welfare Party (formerly the National Salvation Party or NSP) of Professor Necmettin Erbakan and with the mainstream Motherland Party. Some members of the family of the late president Turgut Özal were close to the Nakşibendis. An offshoot of this latter group, the Süleymancıs (followers of Süleyman Hilmi Tunahan (1888–1959), run hostels for boarding school students.

A second influential brotherhood is that of the Nurcus (Followers of Light). Although the Nakşibendis trace their history back to the fourteenth century, the Nurcus appeared only recently as a result of the teaching of the Kurdish shaykh, Said-i Nursi (1876–1960), who sought to bring Islamic inspiration to modern society. The current president of the republic Süleyman Demirel has contributed to Nurcu publications.

Religion, which Atatürk had kept at arm's length, has become respectable once again. There are prayer halls in parliament, ministries, colleges, and other official and unofficial institutions. Leading members of right-wing or center-right parties make a point of attending Friday prayers and of fasting during the Ramazan (Ramadan).

A modus vivendi has emerged between the secular state, as represented by the political establishment, and mainstream, official Turkish Islam. The state subsidizes and otherwise supports official Islam, while the latter recognizes the autonomy of the state and serves it as an instrument of solidarity and social control. Within this framework, there is respect and toleration of personal beliefs and practices, so long as they do not threaten public order.

Yet not everyone is satisfied with the emerging compromise, and the religious question has not been removed from the political arena. The modern, secularized section of society feels threatened by religion. It ascribes toleration to itself and fanaticism to the religious revivalists. However that may be, the well-to-do, particularly in metropolitan areas, find it easy to be tolerant. But tolerance comes hard to those who feel the material and spiritual discomfort of rapid, and perforce uneven, social and economic change.

Militant atheism is rare and confined to a fringe of freethinkers, Marxists and former Marxists. But the military's suppression of Marxist militancy in 1971 and 1980, and the ensuing official encouragement of Islam as an antidote, has created more room for militant Islam.

Fundamentalism represents only a small part of a wider movement, which is more accurately designated "Islamist." Its main current political expression is the Welfare Party, which campaigns for an undefined "just order," accompanied by xenophobic and, in particular, anti-American and anti-Semitic pronouncements. With the virtual disappearance of Marxism as a political force (although the intellectual hangover still lingers), Islamism is the only ideology that challenges the current political system. Its primary appeal is, naturally, to the disadvantaged. A recent survey of Islamist university students has confirmed that they come from poorer, less educated, and more provincial backgrounds than their secularist counterparts.[20]

The Welfare Party has been most successful in poor, suburban metropolitan neighborhoods and in provincial cities, particularly in central and eastern Anatolia. It received 17 percent of the total poll in the last parliamentary elections in October 1991. Although its vote was swollen by the support of extreme nationalists, with whom it campaigned (but from whom it later parted company), its successes in subsequent local government by-elections suggests it could advance further, particularly in conditions of economic hardship and political disorientation. According to provisional results, the Welfare Party received 19 percent of all votes cast in elections to provincial councils on March 27, 1994. The Welfare Party did even better in mayoral elections, where it won control of the metropolitan areas of Istanbul and Ankara previously governed by the Social Democrats.

It would be wrong, however, to classify all voters for the Welfare Party as convinced Islamists, let alone fundamentalists. The party is often credited with good administration in the municipalities it controls. As an opposition party, it is less tainted with corruption than are some of its secularist rivals. It has a highly motivated organization and is good at getting out the vote. Nevertheless, it does not represent all pious Muslims, many of whom support mainstream parties.

At the other end of the political spectrum, secularism draws its support from more than the sophisticated and the affluent. The Turkish Shi'ite (Alevi) community, unlike its Iranian counterpart, is a strong supporter of the secular character of the republic for fear of being dominated by the Sunni majority.

Four different communities are all lumped together as "Alevis" (followers of the Caliph Ali). The most numerous subgroup of Shi'ites are ethnic Turks, who live mainly in central Anatolia. There are also Kurdish Shi'ites, Arab Shi'ites (Nusairis in the province of Hatay), and a community of Azerbaijani Shi'ites. The first three subgroups are generally poorer than their Sunni neighbors and tend to support left-of-center parties.

In central and eastern Anatolia tension between Sunnis and Alevis is endemic. In the late 1970s a number of anti-Alevi pogroms were carried out, the most notorious of which took place in the southeastern city of Kahramanmaraş in December 1978, when more than 100 people were killed. The disturbances in the eastern city of Sivas in July 1993, sparked by a speech by the Turkish publisher of Salman Rushdie's *Satanic Verses*, cost the lives of several Alevi intellectuals, who were among the 37 victims of a fire started by a mob of Sunni fanatics.

Support for secularism in Turkey is thus not confined to a thin upper crust, as is the case in some other Muslim countries. This was made clear when a crowd of several hundred thousand mourners turned into a secularist demonstration the funeral of the radical, secularist newspaper columnist Uğur Mumcu, who was assassinated by Islamist terrorists in Ankara in January 1993. That murder, like previous murders of prominent secularist intellectuals, was almost certainly carried out by terrorists trained in, or funded by, Iran.

Turkish Islamism tends toward the angry expression of social discontent. But although outbreaks of mob fanaticism punctuate Turkish history, assassinations are a recent phenomenon, inspired and usually organized from abroad. In the turbulent 1970s, when Marxists and nationalist racists murdered each other, indigenous Islamists had a comparatively clean record, and the youth organization of the National Salvation Party (known as Akıncılar, or "Raiders") was less bloodthirsty than the Grey Wolves (or "Idealists") on the Right and the revolutionaries on the Left. The Iranian Shi'ite tradition of assassination is alien to Turkey.

The religious question in Turkey is complex. It mirrors social as well as ideological and confessional divisions. It is both a political struggle and a Kulturkampf. It has as much in common with the division between secularists and clericals that followed the French Revolution as it has with the consequences of modernization in the lands of Islam. What distinguishes Turkey from other Islamic countries is not only the strength of secularists but the emergence of a broad common ground, secured both by tolerance and growing secular indifference.

A tradition of statecraft circumscribes the dangers of religious and other ideological enthusiasms. So does a tradition of state Islam, which could also be described as the Islam of army chaplains. "What is good for the country is good Islam," Mustafa Kemal (Atatürk) declared in 1920 in the middle of the War of Independence. Most Turks would say "amen" to that today.

Looking to the future, organic secularization seems to be a stronger force than the Islamic reaction to it. So far, Turkey has followed European trends and fashions, sometimes remarkably quickly, as when the student riots in Paris in May 1968 preceded by only a few weeks the beginning of student militancy in Turkey. Among the affluent in Turkey, as more generally in Europe, one can already see a tolerant religion within a context of secular indifference. But it will be a long time before the whole of Turkish society can reach West European levels of affluence. Until then, social tensions will continue to be mirrored in the religious scene.

These internal tensions can be exacerbated not just by the example of Islamic fanaticism in the Middle East but more so by the West's perceived double standards in dealings with Muslims. The failure of the West to shield the Muslims of Bosnia and Azerbaijan from their local Christian enemies gives ammunition to xenophobic Muslims in Turkey.

The response to the condition of the Palestinians is more complicated. Sympathy for them as fellow Muslims is tempered by widespread distrust, and sometimes downright dislike, of Arabs. Here, memories of Arab "treachery" in World War I are reinforced by current conflicts of interest between Turkey and its Arab neighbors. The fact that Turkish Islamists are believed to be supported by Middle Eastern governments (of Saudi Arabia, Libya, and Iran for different factions) does not endear them to the bulk of their fellow Turks.

Paradoxically, Turkish Islamists draw much of their money from Germany, where Turkish guest workers become fervent Muslims in response to the discomforts of migrant life and under whose liberal constitution extremists of all kinds enjoy much more freedom than they have in Turkey. True, some of the money coming from Germany may also have been donated in the first place by Middle Eastern governments. But it adds to the European dimension of Turkey's religious question.

Important as these external factors are, however, Turkey's ability to negotiate its development at home will determine how much anger spills over into the religious domain. The rulers of Turkey can be left to cope with their religious fanatics. What the West can do — by its trade and investment, no less than by its security policy at home and foreign policy abroad—is to facilitate the creation in Turkey of a comfortable society, which will practice a comfortable form of Islam. Fairness and tact in relations with Muslims throughout the world will, of course, also help.

The attitude of Turks toward non-Muslims in their own country is still influenced by the tradition that equated Turk with Muslim. Non-Muslims are expected to know their place and to refrain from any attempt to convert Muslims. They are then treated with respect. Nevertheless, there is distrust of priests and ministers who tend to be suspected of subverting Turkish society. Greek and Armenian Christianity is viewed as a form of (anti-Turkish) Greek and Armenian nationalism. Nevertheless, blasphemy against any "divine religion" (in effect the religions of the Peoples of the Book—Islam, Christianity, Judaism, and "Sabaeanism"—as defined in the Qur'an) is an offense. Proselytizing sects, such as Jehovah's Witnesses, face difficulties. Enlightened society now accepts Turkish Muslim women who marry non-Muslims. Non-Muslim wives of Muslims are positively welcomed. Again, among the enlightened, there are signs of nostalgia for the religious diversity of late Ottoman times.

In the worst cases, secularist distrust of all religions is grafted onto Muslim distrust of non-Muslims. At best, secularist indifference to religion strengthens traditional tolerance of all Peoples of the Book. In any case, no follower of a "respectable" religion need be embarrassed to practice his faith in Turkey. The law, of course, proclaims the freedom of belief and unbelief.

6

Joining the Rich

On April 14, 1987, Turkey applied for full membership in the European Community. On December 18, 1989, the Commission of the European Community in Brussels advised that opening negotiations would serve no useful purpose, as the EC was not ready to enlarge nor was Turkey ready for membership. Instead, the Commission recommended that links between the two sides should be strengthened in the framework of the treaty of association that they had concluded in 1963. The Commission's advice was accepted by the Council of the Community on February 5, 1990.

The situation has not changed materially since that date. A package of measures, involving the release of credits by the EC—or since late 1993, the European Union (EU)—and intended to promote EU-Turkish relations, has been blocked by Greece. On the other hand, permanent machinery for political consultation was established in December 1992, when Turkey became an associate member of the West European Union, the embryonic defense arm of the then EC. At the same time Turkey reaffirmed its intention to complete a full customs union with the EC in 1995, as envisaged in the treaty of association. That treaty had also looked forward to the free circulation of labor, but the

EC withdrew from its commitment to allow free access to Turkish workers as of December 1986. Moreover, member states of the EC introduced, one after another, visas for prospective Turkish travelers exempted earlier under an agreement reached under the auspices of the (separate) Council of Europe in Strasbourg.

The visa requirement, which is not easily met, is often viewed by Turks as manifesting Turkey's exclusion from the European Union or, more generally, from Europe. Yet, apart from the fact that the EU is not coterminous with Europe, this conclusion is wrong. Turkey has, it is true, been excluded for the foreseeable future from the central decision-making institutions of the EU; but it is not, indeed cannot be, excluded from Europe.

In 1993, 45 percent of Turkey's foreign trade (47 percent of exports and 44 percent of imports) was carried on with member states of the EC, Germany being, by far, Turkey's most important single trading partner. The majority of tourists (and the overwhelming majority of paying tourists, excluding carpetbaggers from Eastern Europe) who visit Turkey come from EC countries. Most of the direct foreign investment in Turkey originates in Europe. More than two-and-a-half million Turkish workers and their dependents reside in Europe—especially in Germany, but also in France, Holland, Belgium, and the Scandinavian countries. Europe attracted most of the 25,000 Turks studying in foreign universities in 1991.

What is at issue is thus not Turkey's relationship with Europe, but the institutional arrangements for it. The richness of that relationship is easily explicable in terms both of history and of geography. Turkey has been part of the European political scene—not only as an external adversary, but also as a factor in intra-European relations—ever since the Ottomans first crossed into Europe in the fourteenth century. The Ottoman Empire was recognized as a member of the concert of Europe at the end of the Crimean War in 1856. When the Organization of European Economic Cooperation (OEEC), the Council of Europe, and

NATO were established in the years following World War
II, Turkey was treated without question as part of Europe.

Nevertheless, although European reservations concerning Turkey are well known, Turkey's "European vocation and commitment to European unity"—to quote the
words of the late Turgut Özal in his letter of application to
the chairman of the Council of the European Community—
also require qualification.[27]

Atatürk's commitment was to contemporary civilization and not to Europe specifically, even though Europe
was seen at the time as the center or at least the most
proximate center of that civilization. After World War II,
the United States guaranteed Turkey's security and provided the bulk of economic aid for its development, and
the American alliance remains to this day the linchpin of
Turkish foreign policy. After the EC decided to defer discussion of Turkey's application for full membership, many
wondered whether Turkey would turn to the Middle East.
In fact, Turkey's relationship with the United States became noticeably closer.

Turkey would certainly like to be recognized as part of
the European Union, but not at the expense of its relations
with advanced industrialized countries outside Europe.
Turkey's membership in the OECD—known as the club of
rich countries, which include the United States, Japan,
Canada, Australia, and New Zealand as well as wealthy
European countries inside and outside of the EU—is a truer
indication of Turkey's aspirations than is the talk of the
country's European vocation.

Nor do the member states of the OECD exhaust the
list of countries against which Turkey would like to measure itself and to which it would like to draw near. The
countries of the Pacific Rim, the members of ASEAN, and,
more recently, China are seen as potentially important
trading partners and are, in some cases and in some measure, sources of inspiration.

Turkey will seek "contemporary civilization" wherever
it manifests itself in material achievement. The hope of the

late president Turgut Özal was not only, or not so much, that Turkey should become part of Europe, but that it should become one of the 10 or 15 leading countries of the world.

When Turkey became an associate member of the EC in 1963, the economy of Europe was expanding. Both Turkey and Greece (which became an associate member at roughly the same time) wanted to benefit from that expansion. After the Cyprus war of 1974, Constantine Karamanlis, who was at the time effective ruler of Greece, decided to seek full membership for political reasons. He hoped to add the weight of Europe to the American alliance, which had guaranteed the security of Greece since 1947, but which had not saved Greeks from the effect of their mistakes in Cyprus. Europe was at the time in recession, following the first oil shock of 1973. Thanks to French support, however, Karamanlis was successful in his bid for full membership.

Until then Turkey had kept step with Greece in seeking aid both from the United States and Europe. But the 1970s were marked by internal troubles and uncertainty in Turkey. Governments changed rapidly as the country battled against terrorism and struggled with a deteriorating economy. Although Turkish diplomats succeeded in safeguarding the main pro-Western orientation of foreign policy, the governments of Bülent Ecevit, the leader of the left-of-center Republican People's Party, were influenced by the neutralist tendencies widespread among the educated classes. These tendencies were reinforced by the arms embargo, which the U.S. Congress had imposed on Turkey after Turkish troops had landed in Cyprus, and by Ecevit's failure to secure sufficient Western aid to pay for his mistakes in economic management. So, far from applying for full membership in the EC, the Turkish government suspended some of its earlier commitments under the treaty of association. It can be argued that had Turkey joined Greece in seeking full membership, both applications would have been refused. The EC would then have been spared the ever-growing cost of integrating Greece and would not have been dragged into the maze of Greek-Turkish arguments.

Turgut Özal made his application in 1987 against the advice of the main members of the EC, particularly of Germany. He almost certainly overestimated Turkey's diplomatic weight and underestimated the EC's resistance to further large calls on its resources. Like Karamanlis after 1974, both Özal and the Turkish political establishment, which supported him in his bid for EC membership, had political considerations in mind. Full membership would, they believed, strengthen democratic institutions in Turkey and Turkey's place in the counsels and the esteem of the West. But Özal was also prompted by economic calculations. Unlike Ecevit in the 1970s, he realized that rapid development of the Turkish economy, which he sought, would require a large and continuing flow of foreign capital. Özal believed that EC membership, which implied the acceptance of laws, rules, and practices necessary for the successful operation of a market economy, would encourage foreign capital to invest in Turkey. Özal saw Turkey's membership as part of the country's integration into the worldwide free-market economy and as a source of funds to facilitate that integration.

As difficulties mounted in negotiations with the EC, the Turkish government lowered its sights. In the last resort, it sought only the EC's commitment to initiate membership negotiations on a specific date. Turkish diplomats indicated that they would be prepared to defer to a distant future the application of the EC rules on the free circulation of labor among the member states. They would be prepared to limit or even to forgo any budgetary transfers from the EC to Turkey. They would be satisfied with the promise of membership, which, the Turkish government believed, would by itself have a favorable effect on the investment climate.

The EC was prepared to confirm Turkey's eligibility for membership, but refused to promise it or to set a firm date for membership negotiations. Brussels realized that were Turkey to become a full member, it would be difficult in the short run, and impossible in the long run, to deny Turkey benefits available to other members. Nor is there any guarantee that Turkey would not come to demand them.

Greek membership has proved costly to Europe. According to OECD figures, net EC transfers to Greece increased every year from 1986 to 1991, totaling U.S.$14.5 billion for the six years.[28] The population of Turkey is nearly six times that of Greece, its GNP per capita more than three times lower in 1991, its agriculture—which is the main beneficiary of EC expenditures—vastly more extensive. If the rules from which Greece has benefited were applied in equal measure to Turkey, the cost to the EC would be prohibitive.

Moreover, at the time of writing, the European Union is in recession. Unemployment is high. Even when growth is resumed, it is likely to be slow. Given current resentment at the presence of foreign workers in European countries, there is no prospect that the EU would allow Turkey's surplus labor freedom of access in the foreseeable future. The formerly communist countries of East and Central Europe are clamoring for European and other outside investment and threatening Europe with their unemployed and underpaid labor. Turkey has, therefore, no choice but to supplement its "European vocation."

Even the promised customs union is problematic. Turkey is already asking for EU help to ease passage to it. Such help, although given to Spain and Portugal as they were accepted for full membership, is unlikely to be given—certainly not in the same measure—to an associate member. A full customs union would also entail rules on state subsidies and other matters, which Turkey would find hard to apply.

It remains, of course, true that, as we have said, Europe is Turkey's largest market and one that lies near at hand. This market will increase in size with the accession of members of the European Free Trade Area (EFTA). Turkey has already negotiated terms with EFTA that replicate, and in some cases improve on, the facilities it enjoys from the EU.

Turkey needs freedom of access to the enlarged, prosperous core of Europe. It will have to reciprocate at least in some measure by opening its market further to European imports. But this purpose could be served by free trade arrangements short of a customs union. Such arrangements would have the further advantage of allowing Turkey more discretion to negotiate preferential tariffs with countries outside Europe.

On the other hand, the advantage of a customs union is that it would more quickly modernize the legal framework within which business operates in Turkey as well as the general structure of the Turkish economy. This would attract foreign investors, including those from third countries (such as Japan) seeking a foothold within the European market. A customs union would also bring some trading benefits, particularly to the Turkish textile industry, the country's main export earner, which would no longer be subject to European import quotas. Other industries, however, could well be damaged by unrestricted European competition.

Above all, a customs union with the European Union is a stage on the road to full membership. For this reason alone, the Turkish government will persist in negotiations to achieve it. But the process will be difficult. The year 1995 may well see the elimination of barriers in the trade in manufactures between Turkey and the European Union. It is unlikely to see the full harmonization of legislation, as envisaged in Brussels. The gap between aspiration and reality will probably be covered by safeguard clauses, which can be invoked for the temporary protection of national interests.

Immediately after the Gulf War, Özal asked for a free trade agreement with United States. His lack of success did not prevent his successors from seeking similar arrangements with Israel. In the last few years, Turkey's determined efforts to attract Japanese investment have met with a fair measure of success. Turkish statesmen and businessmen have also looked for opportunities in the countries of the Pacific Rim. In the first quarter of 1993, China and Taiwan suddenly emerged as an important market for Turkish exports. Together they bought Turkish goods valued at some U.S.$300 million – slightly more than the United States bought during the same period and much more than any other single country, with the exception of Germany.

The main attraction of Europe – for Turkey as for others – lies in the fact that it is a collection of rich countries. But other countries are turning up in the league of the wealthy. Turkey seeks to join them. It will not turn its back on Europe, yet it will not neglect opportunities elsewhere. Although Turkey needs and wants Europe as a partner, it will not restrict its choice of partners to Europe.

7

The Turkic World

Today approximately 120 million people speak Turkic languages around the world. There are some 50 million in Turkey (allowing for 10 million speakers of minority languages out of a population of 60 million); 47 million in the former Soviet Union (1989 census); 12 million in Iran, Afghanistan, and Iraq; and 9 million in China. The remainder are mainly in various European countries.[29]

Turkic-speakers have a perception of common origin. They also have a common religion, because the overwhelming majority of them are, at least nominally, Muslims. Except for the 7 million or so Azerbaijanis and a presumed 20 percent of the population of Turkey, all of whom profess the Shi'ite form (or rather forms) of Islam, the remaining Turkic-speaking Muslims are Sunni.

For a long time, Turkey was the only independent Turkic-speaking state and, as such, the repository of the Turkic tradition of statecraft. It is still by far the strongest Turkic state.

As soon as they achieved independence, the leaders of the Turkic-speaking republics of Azerbaijan, Turkmenistan, Uzbekistan, Kyrgyzstan, and Kazakhstan declared that they would give priority to Turkey in their foreign relations. The same sentiment was expressed by Turkic-speakers who live in autonomous republics in the Russian federation, notably the 7 million Tatars, 1.5 million Bashkirs, and the Muslims of the northern Caucasus (not all of whom are Turkic-speakers).

The leaders of the five independent Turkic republics of the former Soviet Union have all visited Turkey, in some cases more than once. So have the leaders of the autonomous republics of Tatarstan and Chechen-Ingushetia, who aspire to independence. A summit meeting of the presidents of independent Turkic-speaking states was held in Ankara in October 1992.

Turkey has responded by hastening to recognize the independence of the five Turkic republics, opening embassies in their capitals, establishing air links with them, and starting an aid program. Under this program, which is now being coordinated by the newly established Turkish International Cooperation Administration (TICA), credits amounting so far to approximately U.S.$1 billion have been extended; 10,000 scholarships have been awarded to students (including military students) from the Turkic republics; technical advice has been provided, and a beginning has been made in establishing Turkish cultural centers in the Turkic republics. Thousands of Turkish businessmen have visited the republics, and some have taken up residence there.

There is in Turkey a tendency to describe all Turkic-speakers simply as Turks (Azerbaijan Turks, Uzbek Turks, et cetera) and their languages as dialects of Turkish. Neither description is strictly accurate. Turkic-speakers do consider themselves part of an extended family, but how cohesive is that family?

Although the frontiers of the Turkic republics were recently fixed (in most cases by the Soviet government), the peoples after which the republics are named have all developed a feeling of separate national identity. Their sense of all-embracing Turkic kinship coexists with a stronger feeling of local nationalism. Uzbeks have clashed with Kyrgyz and with Turkish deportees from Georgia, and Turkmens have clashed with Turkic-speakers from the Caucasus. Contrary to the claims of advocates of Turkic solidarity, these clashes have not been engineered by malevolent outsiders.

As for the languages, these belong to the same family, and, as a result, the speaker of one Turkic language finds it easy to learn another Turkic language. But in the absence of special linguistic training, these languages are not readily mutually intelligible. In some cases, rough and ready communication can be established (as between Turks and Azeris), in others, it is virtually impossible (as between Turks and Kyrgyz), unless the interlocutor's language is studied expressly.

All the Turkic languages have been grammatically and orthographically fixed under Soviet rule, and this has not only accentuated, but perpetuated differences between them. Although there is talk today of developing a common Turkic language, this makes as little sense as developing a common German-Dutch-Danish language.

In the 1930s, the Soviet government forced all its Turkic-speaking subjects to use the Cyrillic script in writing their native tongues. Today, Turkey is advising all Turkic-speakers to use the Latin alphabet (with orthographic rules developed in Turkey). Only Azerbaijan and Uzbekistan have agreed in principle, although even there, the change from Cyrillic to Latin will take time. The present rulers of Kazakhstan fear that a switch to the Latin alphabet would introduce a further division among their ethnically mixed citizens, many of whom are of Slavic origin. The other two independent Turkic republics are deferring a decision, at least officially, on grounds of expense.

There are also historic differences. Turkey and the Turkic-speaking republics of the former Soviet Union lack the Ottoman past that Turkey shares with the Arabs and Balkan Muslims. But they are linked by the long process of secularization that the elites of both Turkey and the Turkic republics have undergone. Secularism came to Turkey largely from France and to the Turkic republics from Russia. But in both cases, European influences have been strong and long-lived. Like Ankara, the capitals of the Turkic republics strike one immediately as European cities.

On the other hand, Turkey has always preserved its independence, even in times of Ottoman weakness, while the Turkic-speakers of the former Soviet Union have been ruled by foreigners for many centuries. Given this difference in outlook, Russia remains the metropolitan power for ex-Soviet Turkic-speakers. Turkey does not look to a center outside its borders. To be sure, the Turkic-speakers of the former Soviet Union have only begun the process of nation building. As time goes by, one can expect the Turkish language and the Turkish example to become more influential, the Russian language and presence less so.

Yet one must not exaggerate. The number of Russians and other Slavs in the Turkic republics is decreasing, but it is safe to assume that many will stay on. Their presence will reinforce the external influence of Russia as a political, economic, and cultural center. Russian influence has diminished: it no longer excludes all other outside influences, but it is still extensive, if not preeminent.

Moreover, geography, like history, cannot be banished. Russia has a common frontier with Azerbaijan and Kazakhstan. Communications radiating from Moscow extend to all the Turkic republics. Turkey has only a tenuous link with the Nakhichevan Autonomous Republic, which is separated from the rest of Azerbaijan by a strip of Armenian territory. Central Asia is, of course, a long way from Turkey.

The cohesion of the Turkic world is also diminished by economic differences and difficulties. Turkey has a developing, Western-style economy, with an adequate consumer goods industry and services sector. It is largely self-sufficient in its food supply and has a growing capacity to export both farm products and consumer goods. The Turkic republics are saddled with excommunist colonial economies specializing in the supply of such specific products as oil, minerals, and cotton and lacking in services and adequate indigenous supplies of food and consumer goods.

At first sight, the economies of the two sides appear complementary. But the Turkic republics lack not only legal, commercial, and financial institutions and skills, but, more important, money. They do have considerable natural resources, but their exploitation and marketing require vast investments Turkey cannot provide.

At present, in spite of the provision of Turkish export credits, Turkish exports to all the republics of the former Soviet Union account for under 5 percent of Turkey's total exports. Two-thirds of Turkey's foreign trade are conducted with the industrialized countries of the OECD, which also provide Turkey with almost all its foreign investments and invisible revenue from tourism and the remittances of migrant workers.

In fact, Turkey relies on its relationship with OECD countries to build up links with the Turkic and other ex-Soviet republics. What Turkey is seeking is the role of an intermediary between OECD countries and its kinsmen in the former Soviet Union. Its main disadvantage in this search is the lack of geographical contiguity. Its advantages are labor costs, which are lower in Turkey than in most OECD countries, and such links of kinship, language, and culture as it has with the Turkic republics, and the consequent good will it enjoys there.

Clearly, most Western and Far Eastern corporations that will deal with the Turkic republics will do so directly. But if some, at least, choose Turkish partners, employ Turkish subcontractors or some Turkish staff, establish regional offices in Turkey or even choose Turkey for their staff holidays, the Turkish economy will benefit and the special relationship between Turkey and the Turkic republics will gain substance. To the extent that it does so, this special relationship will also enhance Turkey's standing in the counsels of the West.

Turkey's relations with the Turkic republics are thus

not an alternative, but a complement to its relations with OECD countries and, in the first place, with the European Union, which accounts for more than 40 percent of Turkey's total foreign trade. The cooperation between Turkey and the Turkic republics will grow as the latter and other former Soviet republics become integrated in the world free market system. Yet the success of cooperative ventures requires the peaceful resolution of conflicts between and within the former Soviet republics. This requirement poses problems for Turkey.

Turkey wishes to draw Armenia into the pattern of regional cooperation for two reasons. First, Armenia lies astride Turkey's communications with Azerbaijan and through Azerbaijan with Central Asia. Second, Armenia's historic grievances against Turkey complicate the latter's relations with the West, particularly with countries like the United States and France where there are important communities of Armenian origin. Economic cooperation would attenuate historic enmity. The fact that land-locked Armenia needs access through Turkey improves the prospects of mutually beneficial cooperation.

Yet developing productive links between Turkey and Armenia is hindered by the latter's attempt to enlarge its territory at the expense of Azerbaijan. The Azeris demand Turkish support in their war with the Armenians over Nagorno-Karabakh, an autonomous region within Azerbaijan, whose Armenian inhabitants had first decided to join Armenia and later unilaterally declared their independence as a cover for union. The Armenians expelled the Azeri minority from Nagorno-Karabakh and then occupied Azeri territory outside the enclave, setting off a flight of more than a million Azeri refugees. Neither limited Turkish aid to Azerbaijan (in the form of military instructors) nor Turkey's official insistence that it wishes to see the dispute solved under international auspices, and its initiatives to this end in international forums, have succeeded in securing Turkey's national interest in developing regional cooperation.

After deciding to sell electricity to Armenia in November 1992, Turkey then had to rescind its decision the following month under pressure from Azerbaijan. And in April 1993, when the Armenians added the Azeri district of Kälbejar to their other conquests in and around Karabakh and prepared to advance further, Turkey banned the transport through its territory of all supplies to Armenia, even humanitarian ones.

The permanent Armenian occupation of Azeri territory between Karabakh and Iran would affect vital Turkish interests. On the basis of internationally recognized frontiers, Armenia's land link with Iran consists of a mountainous strip, known as Zängezur, through which road communications are difficult to establish. If the Armenians were to keep the low-lying area to the east of Zängezur, which they occupied in the second half of 1993, not only would this widen the obstacle separating Turkey from Azerbaijan and from Turkic republics east of the Caspian, but it would also make it easier for Armenia to enter into a spoiling alliance with Iran to divert part at least of the trade of the Turkic republics from Mediterranean outlets to the Persian Gulf. Such an alliance would have the support of at least some elements in Russia, who wish to maintain a foothold in Transcaucasia and are loath to see that area drawn into a Turkish co-prosperity sphere.

If the Armenian gains threaten to become permanent, Turkey would thus have strong reasons to intervene. But intervention would affect relations with the West, where the memory of Armenian sufferings at the hands of the Turks in World War I is still strong, and hardly anyone knows about the sufferings of the Turks at that time.

Turkey's dilemma would, of course, be eased if the West were more active and more successful in resolving regional disputes. A perception of Western evenhandedness, particularly on issues between Christians and Muslims, is necessary if Turkey's current policy is to succeed.

Critics of Turkish policy accuse it of trying to revive

Pan-Turkism (also called Pan-Turanianism), which arose at the turn of the century and aimed at creating a single state to embrace all speakers of Turkic languages. In particular, Armenian nationalists accuse Turkey of wishing to eliminate them from their homeland to achieve such a Turkic state. Without going into historical arguments, one can say with certainty that all but a handful of Turkish politicians are convinced that the realization of the Pan-Turkist dream is today neither possible nor desirable. As for Turkish public opinion, it sympathizes with Turkic kinsmen and more generally with Muslims abroad, while being overwhelmingly interested in economic development at home. Turkish nationalism, as developed by Atatürk, is local in orientation. So is the nationalism of the newly independent Turkic republics.

The experience of the Arab and Latin American states suggests a parallel. Neither the Arab League nor various associations of Latin American states have ever acquired much substance. There is, of course, this difference: the Turkish republic is a natural leader of the Turkic states, whereas in both the Arab world and Latin America no single state can claim preeminence. Nevertheless, even if an association of Turkic states were to be formed, its capacity for common action would be slight.

Contrary to speculation in the world media, the Turkish government has insisted that it is not competing with any other state in fostering links with its Turkic kinsmen. Certainly, Turkey cannot by itself diminish the role of Russia, which will loom large in the foreseeable future in both the economy and the politics of newly independent Turkic states.

In the closing months of 1993, Turkey repeatedly drew the attention of the West to the danger of reimposed Russian domination in Transcaucasia, where Georgia and Azerbaijan have reversed their original decision not to join the Commonwealth of Independent States (CIS). Moreover, defeat at the hands of the Armenians had led to the downfall of the nationalist and pro-Turkish president of Azerbaijan Abulfäz Elçibey and his replacement by Häydär Aliyev, a former member of the Soviet Politbureau. In spite of widespread suspicions that forces within Russia had a hand in the successes of Armenians in Azerbaijan and of Abkhazians in Georgia—successes that had forced the two countries to seek Russian protection within the CIS—Turkey failed to mobilize countervailing Western pressure. In any case, Turkey's opposition to a Russian return to Transcaucasia was balanced by a desire to maintain good working relations with Russia. If the West did nothing to stop the Russians, Turkey, too, neither would nor could do it. Although competition with Russia is beyond Turkey's means, competition with some other states, notably Iran, is inevitable.

In the independent Muslim states around them, the Turkic republics see a multiplicity of models. The scale stretches from Turkey, a secular republic ruled by parliament, to Iran, an Islamic republic ruled by the clergy. In between lie Saudi Arabia, an Islamic monarchy ruled by lay kings and princes; Pakistan, an Islamic republic, ruled sometimes by parliament and sometimes by the army; and Egypt, where Islam is the state religion and the rulers have been established by the armed forces.

In the eyes of members of the political class in the Turkic republics, whether Communists who have become nationalists or old-time nationalists (who achieved a short-lived hold on power only in Azerbaijan), the Turkish model—or rather the Turkish model of some 50 years ago, before parliamentary rule became a reality—is the most attractive. As in Atatürk's Turkey, power in the Turkic republics is in the hands of those who take a secular, centrist, and modern approach. Given that secular education is much more widespread in the Turkic republics than it had been in Atatürk's Turkey, and that European influences, transmitted through Russia, are well established, Islamic fundamentalism, as practiced in Iran and Saudi

Arabia, has a limited appeal. True, it is likely to be fed by
social dislocation and may become more acceptable in the
shape of Turkish Islamic nationalism (the "Turkish-Islamic
synthesis"), as developed in Turkey. But the feeling of national identity is crucial.

It is because the Tajik language is basically little more
than a dialect of Persian that many Tajiks have been drawn
to the regime in Tehran. The link is not so much Islam as
Iranian kinship. Similarly, a feeling of Turkic kinship will
always be an obstacle between the Turkic republics and
Iran, irrespective of the regime in Iran. There are also specific points of friction between Turkic and Iranian nationalism: the aspiration of Azerbaijani nationalists to the union
of northern (independent) and southern (Iranian) Azerbaijan; the existence of (Iranian) Tajik minorities in Uzbekistan, of an Uzbek minority in Tajikistan, and of a Turkmen
minority in Iran.

Given, however, that the main aspiration of the newly
emancipated Turkic republics is for a reasonable standard
of living and that fundamentalism tends to be a product
material misery, the main competition between foreign role
models will be in providing or facilitating material assistance. Neither Turkey nor Iran is able to provide sufficient
aid on its own. But Turkey is in a much better position
than Iran to act as a channel for Western capital and skills.
To the extent that the Turkic republics need a friend in the
court of the West, Turkey can discharge this function
much better than Iran. Moreover, the political class in the
Turkic republics believes that Turkey is a more advanced
country than Iran.

True, Turkey's role in the Turkic republics should not
be exaggerated. Other countries—Japan, Korea, China, Pakistan, India, Saudi Arabia, Oman, Israel, and of course the
industrialized countries of the West—have already made
contacts and in some cases established joint ventures in
Transcaucasia and Central Asia. But neither should Turkey's influence be discounted. It will, in any case, be stronger

than Iran's. Turkey and Iran now compete in the areas of politics, culture, and the economy – in the last instance particularly in communications and telecommunications.

As mentioned earlier, the Iranian theocratic model has little support in the Turkic republics. In foreign relations, the anti-American and generally anti-Western promptings of the present regime in Iran run contrary to the desire of the Turkic republics to benefit from Western capital, skills, and aid. Imprisoned for over 70 years in the closed communist system, the Turkic republics wish to open up to the whole outside world. They do not wish to exchange the communist prison for isolation within an Islamic, let alone an Iranian, system.

In culture, the advocacy of the Arabic script, not only by Iran, but also by Saudi Arabia and Pakistan, is unlikely to be successful, if only because that script does not suit Turkic phonetics. Its acceptance would also impede contacts with the advanced world.

In communications, however, Iran does offer an alternative to the northern route through Russia. Although, the Russian route will almost certainly continue to be used most frequently, the Turkic republics do seek an alternative, because in some cases a route to the south of Russia would afford a shorter passage to world markets.

Conscious of its geographical advantage, the regime in Tehran has done its best to obstruct transit trade from Turkey to the Turkic republics. Turkish efforts to win over Iran to the idea of regional cooperation have been fruitless. These efforts have been deployed both bilaterally and within the Economic Cooperation Organization – an ineffective forum in which Turkey, Iran, and Pakistan have been joined by the Muslim republics of the former Soviet Union.

The choice of access routes is particularly important in marketing the oil, natural gas, and other mineral resources of Azerbaijan and Central Asia, resources crucial for the development of the area. Although the main export routes will continue to run through Russia, alternative routes will almost certainly be established. Moreover, the Russian route involves certain difficulties.

Soviet oil and gas were transported to Eastern Europe, and thence to the West, by pipeline. Now these pipelines have to cross the newly independent states of Belarus and Ukraine, which will want to augment their transit revenue to cover the increased cost of Russian energy supplies.

Some Soviet oil used to reach foreign markets by sea. Where the southern route was used, the oil was transported in tankers that had to negotiate the Turkish straits on their way to the Mediterranean. It has been debated whether to increase this traffic when oil production in the former Soviet republics is stepped up with the help of Western capital and know-how. But Turkey is arguing that this would present an unacceptable ecological risk to the large and growing urban sprawl of Istanbul.

It is true that the Montreux Convention of 1936, which governs the use of the Turkish straits, provides for the unrestricted passage of commercial ships in peacetime. But, as the country responsible for implementing the convention, Turkey has been regulating this traffic on grounds of safety. For example, it has on occasion closed the straits to other traffic to allow extra-large ships to pass through. The Turkish Ministry of Foreign Affairs has already made it clear that it cannot countenance an increase in oil tanker traffic through the straits. Even if the Montreux Convention prevents a ban, Turkey apparently can make ships wait until the passage is clear, thus raising the cost of transport by tanker to an uneconomic level. In the long run, Turkey could also ask for the convention to be revised in line with modern notions of environmental protection.

One way of cutting out the straits would be to build terminals on the northern coast of Turkish Thrace (or in Bulgaria) and then pipe the oil to terminals on the Aegean coast of Greece or Turkey. The pipeline would be short and therefore comparatively cheap to build. But transferring the oil twice—from ship to pipeline and then back again—would add to transport costs. The same objection would

apply if the sea/land route were shifted further east and if
oil were moved by tanker across the Black Sea from the
Russian port of Novorossisk to the Turkish port of Samsun, and then by a new pipeline to the existing Turkish oil
terminal at Yumurtalık on the Mediterranean.

The alternative Turkey prefers is a route running from
Central Asia across the Caspian Sea to Azerbaijan and
then either through a strip of Armenian territory or through
Georgia to Turkey and the West. Inside Turkey, the new
pipeline would join the existing pipeline from the Kirkuk
field in northern Iraq to Yumurtalık. Azeri officials want
the pipeline to go through Iran to avoid Armenian territory
before entering Turkey. Yet the Turks know from experience that they cannot rely on Iranian cooperation.

Western oil companies also wish to bypass Iran. The
construction of a pipeline through Iran could be avoided by
means of swap arrangements. Azeri and Central Asian oil
could be delivered to Iran and an equivalent quantity of
Iranian oil could be shipped to world markets from terminals in the Persian Gulf. But swap arrangements could
affect only a small part of the hoped-for large increase in
the oil output of Azerbaijan and the Turkic republics of
Central Asia. The bulk of increased oil production would
have to be transported by pipeline, ship, or a combination
of the two.

At present, the Kurdish insurgency in eastern Turkey
rules out any investment on pipelines in the area. After
the Azeri-Armenian conflict and the ambivalent policies of
Iran, the PKK terror campaign in Turkey has become a
third reason for moving the proposed pipeline further west.

The choice of routes for transporting the hydrocarbon
exports of the former Soviet Union looms large in the concerns of Turkish foreign-policy and economic planners.
Given that the ex-Soviet republics are desperate for export
revenue, decisions on large investments both in extraction
and transportation will have to be made soon. The decisions, once made — by the countries where the hydrocarbons
originate, by Western (and Far Eastern) investors, and by

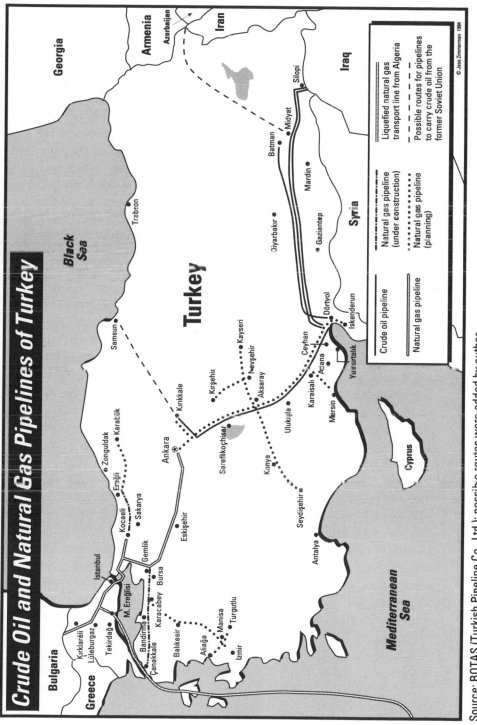

Crude Oil and Natural Gas Pipelines of Turkey

Georgia

Armenia

Azerbaijan

Iran

Iraq

Syria

Bulgaria

Greece

Cyprus

Black Sea

Mediterranean Sea

Turkey

Trabzon

Samsun

Zonguldak

Karatük

Ereğli

Kocaeli

Sakarya

İstanbul

Gemlik

Bursa

M. Ereğlisi

Karacabey

Bandırma

Çanakkale

Tekirdağ

Lüleburgaz

Kırklaréli

Balıkesir

Aliağa

Manisa

İzmir

Turgutlu

Eskişehir

Ankara

Kırıkkale

Sereflikoçhisar

Konya

Seydişehir

Antalya

Kırşehir

Nevşehir

Kayseri

Aksaray

Ulukışla

Karaisalı

Mersin

Adana

Ceyhan

Yumurtalık

İskenderun

Dörtyol

Diyarbakır

Batman

Midyat

Silopi

Mardin

Gaziantep

© Jess Zimmerman 1994

Crude oil pipeline

Natural gas pipeline

Natural gas pipeline (under construction)

Natural gas pipeline (planning)

Liquefied natural gas transport line from Algeria

Possible routes for pipelines to carry crude oil from the former Soviet Union

Source: BOTAŞ (Turkish Pipeline Co., Ltd.); possible routes were added by author.

transit countries—will affect the pattern of trade and economic benefits accruing from it for a long time to come.

After reaching a provisional and precarious agreement on pipeline construction with Azerbaijan and Turkmenistan on the one hand and Western oil companies on the other, Turkey is now trying to salvage it by enlisting Russian support. The choice of the Novorossisk-Samsun-Yumartalık route (bypassing the Kurdish areas) would divide between Russia and Turkey the benefit in, and control over, the shipment of Transcaucasian and Central Asian oil. But would Russia be willing to share with Turkey a trade in which the former Soviet Union once had the sole benefit?

In Moscow, thinking is inevitably confused. Although Moscow has a strong pro-Armenian, thus anti-Turkish, lobby and harbors fears of Turkish expansionism, voices are also heard stressing the benefits of Turkish friendship. At least in theory, there is no reason why Turkey and Russia should not reach an understanding in the matter of transporting hydrocarbons and why such an understanding should not bring some benefits to Turkey. But time and perseverence will be required.

In the case of natural gas, there is an economic advantage in uninterrupted land transportation, which is provided by the existing pipelines going overland to Western Europe. An additional route through Transcaucasia and Turkey might become possible some time in the future, even though Armenians, Iranians, and Kurds prevent it now.

Iran is not, of course, an obstacle to telecommunications, a sector in which Turkey made much progress in the 1980s, when it also established manufacturing facilities under license from foreign corporations, such as Northern Telecom of Canada, Siemens of Germany, and Alcatel of France. Turkey has lost no time in donating telephone exchanges to, and establishing joint ventures in, telecommunications with the Turkic republics. It has already made some progress toward its aim of ensuring that the Turkic republics should be linked to world telecommunications systems via Turkey.

Western governments and private corporations are rightly seeing in Turkey a promising partner in the development of the Asian republics of the former Soviet Union. But the full potential of the promise will only be fulfilled if regional conflicts are resolved and Turkey can stabilize its economy as well as pacify its Kurdish areas.

8

A Regional Power

For nearly 40 years Turkey served as the southeastern bastion of the NATO alliance. Today it remains a member of the alliance. But the end of the cold war, followed by the disintegration of the Soviet Union, whose threat NATO had countered, reduces the need for a defensive bastion. Now Turkey claims a new role.

As the disciplines of the cold war were lifted, a vast area of instability came into being. It stretches from the EU countries in the West to the Pacific region in the East. It also includes much of the Middle East, which has been unable to achieve a stable order since the end of World War II. Formerly a peripheral bastion of NATO, Turkey now lies at the center of a new area of instability. Geographically, it is well placed to serve as a base from which a new order could radiate.

First as prime minister and then as president, Turgut Özal controlled the government of Turkey from the end of 1983 until the elections of October 1991. He was well aware of the role that his country could play in a rapidly changing regional scene and did much to propagate the concept of Turkey as an island of stability in a troubled sea. Süleyman Demirel, who became prime minister in November 1991 and was elected president in May 1993, has sought to spread the same message.

Like the late Turgut Özal, Demirel believes that it is not enough for Turkey to enjoy stability within its own borders. Turkey will not be able to ensure, or safely enjoy, its own stability unless international order also extends to its neighbors. The Turkish authorities would find it much easier to master the problem posed by Kurdish and, to a lesser extent, Islamic and revolutionary Marxist terrorism, if the regimes in Damascus, Baghdad, and Tehran abided by international law and did not seek to profit from terrorism. It is therefore in Turkey's interests to assist efforts to establish law and order outside its borders. By itself, Turkey cannot bring order to the Balkans, the neighboring republics of the former Soviet Union, and the Middle East. But it can make a significant contribution to international, especially Western, efforts in this direction. The belief that Turkey is now strong enough to be considered a regional power is widely held in Turkey, even if not all Turks see a benefit in exercising this power.

The Gulf crisis that erupted after the Iraqi invasion of Kuwait in August 1991 gave President Özal the opportunity to place his country firmly in the allied coalition, which was formed to uphold international law. Özal did not hesitate to take part in blockading of Iraq—the country from which Turkey procured most of its crude oil, with which it had flourishing economic relations, and through which it conducted its trade with the Gulf countries.

Overcoming considerable domestic opposition, Özal secured from parliament permission to send troops abroad and to allow the stationing of foreign troops on Turkish soil. As it turned out, no Turkish troops took part in the fighting. The president favored at least a token military contribution, but the military high command used every argument to dissuade him. Even so, the fear of a Turkish military intervention tied down a considerable part of the Iraqi army on the Turkish frontier. A more direct contribution was made by the use of joint NATO bases in southern Turkey for offensive operations by allied war planes.

Turkey asked for NATO aid to ward off the retaliation that Saddam Hussein had threatened, and a token force of aircraft was sent to Turkey by the European members of NATO. The hesitation, particularly on the part of Germany, to meet Turkey's request was justified on the grounds that the Gulf War was, as far as NATO was concerned, an out-of-area operation. It thus became clear that any new role Turkey might play in the region would require redefining the role of NATO or providing some new aegis for Turkish actions. Turkey would prefer NATO to assume new responsibilities, as it has done to a limited extent in former Yugoslavia.

One reason why Özal's forward policy in the Middle East met strong opposition at home was that it went against the principle that Turkey should not take sides in inter-Arab disputes. This principle had once before been breached, when Turkey became a founding member of the Baghdad Pact against the opposition of Gamal Abdel Nasser's Egypt. But the collapse of the Baghdad Pact, after the fall of the Iraqi monarchy in 1958, and of its successor, the Central Treaty Organization (CENTO), after the fall of the Iranian monarchy in 1979, seemed to vindicate the wisdom of keeping out of Middle Eastern alignments.

President Özal had hoped that by siding unequivocally with the United States, he would not only minimize the losses Turkey would suffer from the conflict, but also gain Turkey a voice in a future Middle Eastern settlement. The first hope was realized as Turkey received compensation, largely in the form of Saudi Arabian oil. Arguably, President Özal's policy secured Turkey a better understanding on the part of its allies of its difficulties in the Kurdish question. But Özal's critics claim that it was allied policy, and Özal's support for it, that exacerbated these difficulties in the first place.

However that may be, Turkey's involvement in the Middle East peace settlement remains slight, and its hopes for the area are largely unrealized. The founders of the Turkish republic tended to see the Middle East as a source of danger rather than benefit for Turkey. The danger has since been exemplified by the vast armory Saddam Hussein amassed with the proceeds of Iraqi oil revenue. This has shaken the feeling of superiority with which the Turkish high command had tended to view Arab armies and has underlined Turkey's defensive interest in the area.

Yet as the wealth of the oil-producing Arab states increased after the oil price rises of 1973, Turkey began to perceive an economic interest in the Middle East. The past 20 years have demonstrated Turkey's ability to export sufficient goods and services to the oil-producing states to cover the cost of imported oil. But they have also shown that Arab capital seeks the highest rate of return available on the world market and that Turkey cannot compete on these terms. Thus while Turkey's trade with the Arabs and Iranians has developed, Arab investment in Turkey has been slight.

One remaining area holds considerable economic potential for Turkey. Ever since the 1970s, Turkey has sought to become a transit route for pipelines transporting Middle Eastern oil and gas to Western markets. A twin pipeline has been built between the Kirkuk oilfield in northern Iraq and the Turkish terminal at Yumurtalık on the Mediterranean Sea. Use of the pipeline was interrupted when the United Nations imposed sanctions against Saddam Hussein. In the meantime there has been no progress with schemes to construct oil and gas pipelines from Iran and the Arab Gulf states or with the project put forward by President Özal to feed water from the Seyhan and Ceyhan rivers in southern Turkey all the way to the Gulf.

The obstacles that block these plans are largely political and derive from the instability of the Middle East and the conflicts in which it is involved. If peace were established from the Mediterranean to the Gulf and if a modus vivendi were achieved with Kurdish nationalists, at least some of these large-scale investment projects could be realized and bring large benefits to Turkey. This is another reason why a Middle East peace settlement is in Turkey's interest.

The building of a water-loading terminal on the Manavgat River in southern Turkey is a case in point. When the press first reported that Turkish water would be shipped by tanker to Israel, angry Arab reaction forced the Turkish authorities to keep the project under wraps. Inhibitions disappeared after the signing of the Israeli-Palestinian peace accord. Turkish water is now openly offered for sale both to Arabs and Israelis.

Yet the interests of Turkey and of its Muslim neighbors to the south and east are not everywhere compatible. There is a conflict of interest in utilizing the waters of the Euphrates and Tigris rivers, which rise in Turkey before they flow to the Arab countries. The more water Turkey retains, the less will be available for irrigation and power generation in Syria and Iraq. Turkey's willingness to sell electricity to its southern neighbors will not eliminate the losses the Turkish southeastern Anatolia project will cause them. Turkey has promised unilaterally to release half the water of the Euphrates River downstream. Syria and Iraq ask for more. Turkey firmly refuses to increase its neighbors' share and to enter into any agreement that might cast doubt on its right to dispose of the water at its discretion. As this refusal is unlikely to change, the water dispute will continue to poison Turkish-Arab relations.

Although Turkey started harnessing the flow of the Euphrates for power generation in 1975, when the Keban dam was completed, it did not use any of the water for irrigation. The Arab states, which were used to receiving the entire flow of the Euphrates and most of the waters of the Tigris, were rudely shocked when the Turkish southeastern Anatolia project put an end to their privileged position. Whatever share of the water Turkey releases downstream, the Arabs will be the losers, as they will no longer have all of it.

Moreover, the construction of pipelines to and through

Turkey can only proceed at the expense of other routes – to the Persian Gulf, the Syrian ports on the Mediterranean, or the Red Sea. The Kirkuk-Yumurtalık pipeline was built because the regimes in Baghdad and Damascus were at loggerheads. In the unlikely event that all Arab states achieve peace with each other, as well as with Israel and Iran, the Turkish route could well be bypassed. But in the case of natural gas, the uninterrupted land route Turkey offers yields an economic advantage.

On a smaller scale, Turkey's current effort to turn Istanbul into a regional business center could damage an Arab offshore banking center such as Bahrain and prevent the revival of Beirut as the commercial capital of the Middle East. In addition to conflicting economic interests, there are actual or potential political conflicts between Turkey and at least some of its Arab neighbors. Syria has not reconciled itself to the loss of the province of Hatay, which was ceded by France to Turkey in 1939.

Until recently, common opposition to Kurdish nationalism provided a bond between Turkey and Iraq that transcended the nature of the Iraqi regime. Turkey felt itself threatened more by Kurdish than by Arab nationalism. But Saddam Hussein's ambitious and adventurous tendencies have changed Turkey's perception of threat. The possibility of an unfriendly Arab state, armed to the teeth with weaponry financed by oil revenue, can no longer be disregarded.

Because the development of the Turkish economy has made Turkey depend more on imported crude oil, the security of oil supplies is an important Turkish national interest. Turgut Özal realized that not only did his country share the U.S. interest in keeping Arab oil out of the clutches of megalomaniac despots, but that its weaker economy made it much more vulnerable to the political use of oil as a weapon.

Until the overthrow of the shah, Turkey could see Iran as a force restraining Arab nationalism. Today, the Islamic Republic of Iran remains, of course, hostile to Arab nationalism. But it is hostile also to the secular system of government established in Turkey by Atatürk. Iranian agents have been involved in the murder of prominent secularists in Turkey. The Turkish government views the Islamic republic as a spoiling, destabilizing force in the Middle East.

Turkey has been and is doing its best to maintain profitable exchanges with Iran. The two countries have lived at peace for three centuries, but genuine cooperation has been rare. Even when the shah was in power, he preferred to bypass Turkey in his dealings with the West. Nothing came of the projects of oil and gas pipelines from Iran to Turkey, because the shah concentrated on exporting direct from the Gulf or supplying natural gas to the Soviet Union. Common membership in the Baghdad Pact, as well as in its successors CENTO and the Regional Cooperation and Development, did little to foster cooperation between Turkey and Iran. Today common membership in the Economic Cooperation Organization is even less important. Turkey and the Islamic Republic of Iran can reach limited agreements, but Iran cannot be depended on, certainly not as a friend of Turkey.

Ankara views Israel as a much more dependable counterweight to Arab nationalism. Turkey recognized the state of Israel immediately after its proclamation. Relations soured when Turkey became a member of the Baghdad Pact, which Israel saw as a threat, but revived in 1958 when Turkey concluded a secret agreement of cooperation with Israel after the fall of the Iraqi monarchy. In the 1960s and 1970s, particularly after the 1970s brought oil wealth to the Arabs, Turkey once again distanced itself from Israel, and diplomatic relations were reduced to chargé d'affaires level. The Palestine Liberation Organization was allowed to set up a diplomatic mission in Ankara, and in 1991 Turkey gave platonic recognition to a Palestinian state.

In official pronouncements, Turkish policy has always been based on UN resolutions and on the principle of opposition to the "acquisition of territorial and political advantages through the use of force." But the most notable example of the use of force in the Middle East was given by Saddam Hussein in 1990, and after the Gulf War, Turkey's relations with Israel became noticeably friendly. Diplomatic relations were restored to ambassador level. Solemn celebrations were held to mark the five-hundredth anniversary of the arrival in Ottoman dominions of Sephardic Jews expelled from Spain. The Turkish authorities and the Jewish community in Turkey cooperated in treating the occasion as a demonstration of the Turkish tradition of religious toleration.

The widening of relations with Israel coincided also with the greater weight given by Turkish policymakers to the American alliance following the failure of Turkey's application for full membership in the EC. Thus, both regional and worldwide considerations underlie the current rapprochement between Turkey and Israel. The events of the past half century have demonstrated that the two countries share solid common ground in the shifting sands of the Middle East.

Although a stable peace settlement in the Middle East is in Turkey's interests, Turkey itself is not prepared to take political risks in the area, certainly not alone, and only to a limited extent in the company of its Western allies. Pending an overall settlement, Turkey's relations with America's friends in the region—Israel, Egypt, Saudi Arabia, and the Gulf principalities—have become closer. But the Middle East is not an area where major initiatives can be expected of Turkey.

Turkey has, however, launched an initiative further north. Even before the Soviet Union had ceased to exist, President Özal proposed that regional economic cooperation should be developed among the riparian countries of the Black Sea and also their immediate neighbors. At first there was talk of setting ambitious economic objectives: the free movement of capital and labor throughout the region, the reduction of customs and other barriers to trade, common sponsorship of major investments, the creation of a regional development bank, et cetera. But it soon became clear that if the new grouping was to bring any benefits at all, these would be mainly political.

The Black Sea Economic Cooperation Region was formally launched at a summit meeting in Istanbul on June 25, 1992. All the states bordering the Black Sea, as well as Moldova, Albania, Greece, Armenia, and Azerbaijan, were represented by heads of state or government. All participants pledged their best efforts to cooperate and agreed to study measures and projects to this end. Since then, Turkish businessmen have been active in the area, mainly in selling consumer goods, which Turkey produces cheaply and which all excommunist countries lack. But the present poverty of excommunist countries limits the market. It limits also the scope for multilateral projects, unless Western or Far Eastern finance can be found. Little local capital exists to circulate or finance a regional bank, and efforts to obtain financing from the London-based European Bank for Reconstruction and Development, the international bank set up to invest in excommunist countries, have produced meager results.

The free circulation of labor within the grouping was never likely: Turkey fears an influx of poor neighbors; Bulgaria fears being swamped by Turks. Greece, which would gladly be rid of the Turkish minority in western Thrace, would certainly never accept an addition to their number.

The Black Sea Economic Cooperation grouping does constitute a convenient forum for the discussion of local bilateral and multilateral problems. It is best viewed as a subgrouping of the CSCE, to which the Black Sea group's opening declaration makes an express reference.[30] After the UN and CSCE, it provides a third venue for Greece and Turkey, Armenia and Azerbaijan (together with their neighbors Turkey and Georgia), and Turkey, Greece, and Bulgaria to work on resolving their conflicts and differences. It reminds neigboring countries of the benefits of cooperation. As such it is a factor, however minor, in stabilizing the Black Sea region and its hinterland.

Even before the Black Sea cooperation initiative was

launched, Turkey had improved relations with Bulgaria to the point where contacts were established between the armed forces of the two countries to bolster mutual confidence. The crisis in relations between the two, which had developed when the Bulgarian Communist dictator Todor Zhivkov attempted forcibly to assimilate the million or so Turks in his country and to expel those who refused to be assimilated, was solved as soon as the Bulgarian Communist regime collapsed.

Bulgarian Turks are now represented in the parliament in Sofia and are active in local politics. Not only have they reverted to their former names, but they have dropped the Slavic forms of Muslim surnames they had used since the formation of independent Bulgaria. They continue to have some grievances, over such matters as the status of Turkish in schools and the property claims of those Bulgarian Turks who have returned from Turkey. But as far as Balkan minorities go, their position, at this time of writing, is enviable. Nevertheless, it would be too optimistic to assume that ethnic hostility between Bulgarians and Turks has vanished, because the size of the Turkish minority, which was reduced by emigration, is bound to grow, given that its birthrate is higher than that of the Bulgarian majority.

Soon after the fall of the communist regime in Albania, Turkey gave some aid to that country and offered military cooperation, particularly in training Albanian officers in Turkish establishments. Contacts developed also between Turkey and the former Yugoslav republic of Macedonia even before the latter proclaimed its independence.

The new links between Turkey on the one hand and Bulgaria, Macedonia, and Albania on the other bred fears of encirclement in Athens, which had earlier cultivated good relations with the communist regimes both in Yugoslavia and Bulgaria. By inviting Greece to take part in Black Sea cooperation, Turkey sought to allay these fears, which, in any case, derive from a misunderstanding of Turkish motives.

Turkey does not seek to revive the Ottoman Empire in

the Balkans or elsewhere. It is of course interested in the welfare of kindred Turks and Muslims in the Balkans, but insists that these should be good citizens of the countries in which they reside and should be treated fairly. When they are not, Turkey appeals to the international community to redress the wrong.

The principle that Turkey does not act alone was emphasized repeatedly by Prime Minister Süleyman Demirel and his ministers in the closing months of 1992, as the sufferings of the Bosnian Muslims increased at the hands of the Serbs. Turkey appealed for action in the UN, CSCE, NATO, the Islamic conference organization, and in bilateral contacts. It repeatedly expressed the fear that Western inaction would leave the clear impression that Christians were not interested in the welfare of Muslims. Turkey warned that the conflicts in former Yugoslavia, as in Nagorno-Karabakh, should not be allowed to assume the form of wars of religion. But when it brought the matter to parliament in December 1992, significantly together with the crisis in Somalia, the Turkish government sought authority to commit Turkish troops abroad only in the context of joint international action.

Persisting ethnic conflicts that involve Christians and Muslims on opposite sides have a destabilizing influence also within Turkey. These conflicts challenge the European, or more generally Western, model, which Mustafa Kemal Atatürk chose when he founded the republic and to which all his successors have remained true. They increase domestic opposition to the Western orientation of Turkish foreign policy and to the secularist basis of its internal policy.

The theory that has shaped the behavior of the Turkish republic assumes that the religious division between Muslims and Christians can be disregarded for most practical purposes. The instances when this theory has been breached inside Turkey have been few. By and large, Turkey has developed steadily to become the only pro-Western or (as many Turks would prefer to call it) European democratic Muslim country.

The ethnic conflicts that pit Muslims and Christians against each other in former Yugoslavia and in other former communist countries, as well as the feeble reaction to them on the part of predominantly Christian Western countries, are bound to strengthen the hand of the minority of Turks who believe that Europeanness and Islam are not after all compatible. If their case is proved for them, both the West and Turkey will be the losers.

Turkey may be developing into a regional power, but for the foreseeable future it can exert its influence only within and through an international system. With all its faults, only the West (as represented in NATO) can provide a security system of any effectiveness. The Islamic conference organization, the new Black Sea regional grouping, the Economic Cooperation Organization (of Turkey, Iran, Pakistan, and the Muslim republics of the former Soviet Union), or any future association of Turkic states could, with luck, become useful adjuncts of international order. But as Ankara realizes, guaranteeing the international order goes far beyond the ability of these organizations.

9

Philhellenes and Turcophiles

The rivalry between Greeks and Turks warps the view
that outside observers, who are neither Greek nor Turkish,
have of Turkey and, to a lesser extent, of Greece. Certainly
since the beginning of the nineteenth century, writers on
Turkish affairs have fitted all too neatly into two classes —
Philhellene or Turcophile. The dichotomy has lasted to this
day. It is time to end it.

The feud with Greece is peripheral to Turkey's main
concerns, which at present involve the aspiration of some
60 million Turkish citizens to a West European standard of
living and their difficulty in coming to terms with Kurdish
nationalism at home. But fear of Turkey rules the political
mind of Greeks as well as Armenians. It creates conscious
or unconscious misapprehensions that influence outsiders — those who, often for generous reasons, sympathize
with Greeks or Armenians, as well as those who have no
foot in either camp.

The feud between Greeks and Turks can be explained
in terms of a long history of conflict. Here are the key
dates: 1071, when the Seljuk Turks defeated the Byzantine
emperor Romanos Diogenes and began the conquest of the
present-day territory of Turkey; 1453, when the Ottoman
sultan Mehmet II conquered the Byzantine capital Constan-

tinople; 1821, when the Greeks in present-day Greece rose against their Ottoman rulers and set about building the modern Greek national state; 1919, when the armies of that national state attempted to conquer western Turkey; 1922–1923, when that attempt was defeated and a population exchange ended the cohabitation of Greeks and Turks, except in Turkish Istanbul, Greek western Thrace, and British-ruled Cyprus; 1955, when Greek nationalists launched a terrorist campaign for the union of Cyprus with Greece, upsetting the Turks both in Cyprus and in Turkey; and 1974, when Turkish troops landed in Cyprus to thwart such a union.

In between these confrontations, Greeks lived peaceably enough with their Turkish neighbors in mixed communities, as was usually the case during the long centuries of Ottoman Muslim rule. Although the end of this peaceful cohabitation was brought about by specific historical events, it was part of a larger pattern of the breakup of multinational empires and the creation among their ruins of more or less homogeneous national states.

The regrouping of Greeks and Turks in their national states ushered in a period of peace and even of reasonably friendly relations, which lasted from 1930, when Greece recognized that the eastern Aegean seaboard was irrevocably lost to it, to 1955, when the Cyprus problem erupted in violence. After World War II, not only did Greece and Turkey have little to quarrel about, they also had good reason to join hands to resist the threat of Soviet expansion. In 1947 they both became beneficiaries of U.S. aid under the Truman Doctrine; in 1950 they both sent troops to Korea; and in 1952 they were both admitted to NATO.

Yet the beginning of the quarrel over the future of Cyprus was followed almost immediately by an anti-Greek riot in Istanbul. It effectively ended the existence of the Greek community in that city and revealed the fires of ethnic hatred still smoldering beneath the surface of good official relations.

The deterioration in relations was halted in 1959 when

the prime ministers of Greece and Turkey agreed on the creation of a bicommunal Cyprus republic, which was duly proclaimed in 1960. But in December 1963, Greek nationalists, who wanted to remove from the republic's constitution the entrenched rights of Turkish Cypriots, attacked the latter, causing many more deaths than had occurred in the Istanbul riot of 1955 and ending for all intents and purposes the cohabitation of Greeks and Turks in mixed communities on the island. Their geographical separation was consummated after the Turkish landings in 1974.

Today virtually no Turks live in the southern two-thirds of the island, which is ruled by the Greek Cypriot government recognized internationally (except by Turkey) as the government of the Republic of Cyprus. Similarly, virtually no Greeks are in the northern third of the island, which constitutes the Turkish Republic of Northern Cyprus, proclaimed unilaterally on November 15, 1983, and recognized to this day only by Turkey.

The brief Cyprus war of July–August 1974 did not turn into a war between Greece and Turkey. But it exacerbated a series of disputes in the Aegean. These concern

• the delimitation of territorial waters. Greece reserves the right to extend the limits from 6 to 12 miles, but Turkey has declared that it would consider such an extension as a casus belli. An extension of Greek sovereignty over virtually the whole of the Aegean Sea would jeopardize free access to Turkey's western coast.
• the delimitation of the continental shelf. Greece maintains that its islands in the Aegean are all entitled to their continental shelf, which would in that case account for almost the entire Aegean seabed, while Turkey claims the continental shelf east of a line bisecting the Aegean, with the exception of the shelf under the 6-mile territorial waters surrounding Greek islands.
• the delimitation of air space: Greece contends that its air space extends 10 miles beyond its coastline (pending

the extension of territorial waters to 12 miles), while Turkey maintains that Greek air space does not go beyond the present 6-mile territorial waters.

• the fortification of Greek islands in the eastern Aegean. Turkey claims it violates the provisions of the treaties of Lausanne (1923) and Paris (1947), while Greece argues that the relevant provisions of the Treaty of Lausanne were abrogated by the convention of Montreux (1936) and that, in any case, the right to self-defense overrides treaty obligations.

• control of NATO defense arrangements, civil aviation, air and sea rescue, and other services. Greece claims such control for the entire Aegean region to the west of Turkey's territorial waters; Turkey wants a half share, although it has chosen not to insist on its claim in some cases.

The dispute over the continental shelf brought Greece and Turkey to the brink of an armed clash in March 1987. Since then, however, the two countries have agreed to disagree, particularly because few material interests are involved and some disputes (for example, over the NATO command structure) have become less important with the ending of the cold war. At present the Cyprus problem is the main and almost the only obstacle to normal relations between the two countries.

The decision of the Turkish government to send troops to Cyprus in 1974, and the parallel decision of the United States not to interdict the landing, have caused lasting trauma in Greece. The Greek feeling of insecurity has been attenuated, but not eliminated, by Greece's admission to the EC on January 1, 1981, and to its embryonic military arm, the West European Union, in November 1992.

The continued presence of Turkish troops in Cyprus is, in Greek eyes, a proof of Turkish expansionism. Greece fears that Turkey will in the future try to push its frontiers forward in Cyprus, in Greek western Thrace, where there are some 120,000 Turks, and in the Balkans, relying on the million or so Turks in Bulgaria and the Muslim Bosnians and Albanians further west.

These Greek fears, to which the Cyprus military operation originally gave rise, are exacerbated by the growing disparity between the populations of the two countries. When the Treaty of Lausanne put an end to hostilities between them in 1923, there were roughly 7 million Greeks to 12 million Turks. Today there are 10 million Greeks and nearly 60 million Turks. Moreover, because the population of Greece is more or less stationary while Turkey's is increasing at a net annual rate of 2.2 percent, the disparity will grow. In a few years, the population of metropolitan Istanbul alone will exceed that of the whole of Greece. Turkey is also outstripping Greece in its rate of economic development, although admittedly it is starting from a much lower baseline. Finally, Greeks fear that the emergence of newly independent Turkic republics in the former Soviet Union will add to the strength and international importance of Turkey.

Although Turkey is undoubtedly growing in strength, the present division of Cyprus is no proof of Turkish expansionism. It is rather a further step in the geographical separation of Greeks and Turks that was effected elsewhere in 1923. Moreover, Cyprus is a special case, because it was expressly set up as a bicommunal state in 1960 and because Turkey, as a coguarantor with Britain and Greece of the 1960 constitutional settlement, had the right to intervene to preserve its bicommunal character. It is true that Turkey's right to intervene could be exercised only for the purpose of reestablishing the 1960 constitution. But that constitution, which had been unilaterally altered by the Greek Cypriots in 1964, could not be restored in 1974.

As for Turks and Muslims in western Thrace and throughout the Balkans, Turkey claims only the right to speak up in their defense when they are oppressed. It relies on international law and, where possible, on international action to stop the oppression. Turkey has shown no sign of wishing to intervene unilaterally, let alone to expand its borders in the Balkans.

The Ottoman Empire had been a multinational, multi-confessional state. The Turks tried and failed to keep it together. They did not initiate the process of ethnic separation in the Balkans, in Cyprus, or in the Near East.

Today the international community is right to condemn the practice of ethnic cleansing. Where an ethnically mixed population exists, common humanity demands that people should not be uprooted or killed on grounds of ethnic identity. But a mixed society that has been destroyed by force cannot be reconstituted, at least not until ethnic hatred has subsided and the wounds of separation have been healed. Fifty years after World War II, no one is advocating that Germans be resettled in Czech Sudetenland or western Poland. The idea that Greeks can be resettled among the Turks of northern Cyprus is similarly impracticable. Any such attempt would inevitably lead to a renewal of the bloodshed that ceased in Cyprus in August 1974.

In Cyprus, in Israel and Palestine, and in the Indian subcontinent, the international community has perversely prolonged disputes by failing to prevent forcible changes and then refusing to recognize them, while being unable to reverse them. It seems likely that the same fate will befall former Yugoslavia.

The Western community, led by the United States, is right to try to resolve the Cyprus dispute. Although the island is at peace and has no refugees who have not been absorbed, the absence of a settlement is an invitation to mischief-makers.

The Western community is wrong, however, to push for a settlement that, to all available evidence, will not work. Recreating an ethnically mixed Cyprus under a federal government will multiply points of friction between Greeks and Turks and is not a sensible goal.

UN Security Council resolutions require that a Cyprus settlement should be just, lasting, and acceptable to both communities. But no mutually acceptable solution has emerged from intercommunal talks that have been going on intermittently since 1964, when a UN peacekeeping force (UNFICYP) was first sent to Cyprus. The Western community should now decide what kind of settlement is likely to last and act accordingly.

Feelings of ethnic animosity subsist on either side of the dividing line in Cyprus. That line is a fire barrier; removing it would be foolhardy. The argument that greater contact will reduce mutual hostility and allow Greeks and Turks to live peaceably in mixed communities is a romantic myth. Greeks in Greece and Turks in Turkey continue to distrust each other, but they can live peacefully side by side because they live in their own states. There is no reason why the same should not be true in Cyprus, where the memories of intercommunal bloodshed are more recent.

A de facto settlement has been in place in Cyprus since 1974. Given that a more durable one cannot be put in its place, the present position should be accepted de jure, with such minor modifications as can be mutually agreed. Relations between Greece and Turkey will then gradually improve, as both parties see the futility of thwarting each other on the wider international stage and the benefit of working together where they have interests in common.

Conclusion

Seventy years after its founding, Turkey must meet an internal challenge before it can play the wider regional role for which its inherent strength equips it. This internal challenge is essentially political.

Since 1950, Turkey has had a freely elected parliamentary government except for three brief interruptions when governments sustained by parliament were seemingly unable to cope with the country's problems. If the military had not intervened, it is sometimes argued, parliament would have been able to find a way out of the difficulties, and the practice of democracy could have been perfected. Now, 10 years after the country's return to parliamentary rule in November 1983, internal problems are once again piling up. Democratic politicians who complain of having been needlessly pushed aside by the military in the past thus have a new opportunity to prove their worth.

Besides addressing its most pressing problems—that is, managing both the economy and Kurdish disaffection—Turkey needs to improve public administration. It must match the management skills of the fast-developing private sector of the economy if it is to meet the requirements of a crowded urban society.

Turkey's fragmented political parties are often blamed

for the shortcomings of parliamentary government. It is, of course, in the nature of political parties to represent the interests of their members and of their electoral constituency. It is in the nature of politicians to promise the earth. But where parliamentary government is effective, political party interests and extravagant promises have to take account of the more general national interest as conceived by a more or less well-informed electorate.

Turkey enjoys at least two advantages in facing its present difficulties. The first is that most electors, including probably most Kurds, believe in the existence of an overarching national interest. Where there are only group interests, parliamentary government is impossible. The second advantage is that after 40 years of free electoral politics, the electorate is acquiring a better grasp of what politicians actually have the power to deliver. With many other countries, however, Turkey faces this danger: the failure of successive elected governments to make good their promises may be discrediting parliamentary politics. The public perception of rampant political corruption increases the danger, opening an opportunity not only to proponents of authoritarian rule but also to irrational forces.

In the 1970s these forces were represented by Marxist revolutionaries on the one side and racist nationalists on the other. Today, believers in a Marxist utopia have all but disappeared, while believers in an Islamic one have grown in numbers. But the danger must not be exaggerated: believers in an Islamic "just order" as the answer to all problems are probably no more numerous in Turkey than are supporters of the Front National in France. The record shows that the majority of Turkish voters support both the practice of democracy and rational democratic policies. Governments and party alignments will change, but there is no reason why the country should not find politicians capable of managing a modern democracy.

True, political skills of a high order are needed in current conditions of economic hardship and ethnic tension.

The advances made by the Welfare Party in local government elections in March 1994, in particular the election of Islamist mayors in Istanbul and Ankara, have shaken Turks who support the secular character of their republic and reawakened fears of religious reaction. Social peace appears to be in danger. But if the past is any guide, the danger will be averted.

There is no reason either to despair of solving the country's economic problems. The economy is much stronger today than in the late 1950s and 1970s when political mismanagement had produced crises of growth. A stabilization program, under whatever name, will inevitably be implemented the moment that the Turkish government fails to find sufficient foreign funds to cover its overspending. In both 1960 and 1980, it fell to the military to deal with the consequences of economic laxity by democratic governments. Today, an economic stabilization program, although it would be unpopular and could spell the doom of the government that introduces it, need not interrupt democratic government as such. The esteem in which democracy is held internationally will encourage democratic forces within Turkey to cope with the popular reaction to economic stabilization.

Once stabilization is achieved, economic growth should become steadier. In average growth, Turkey has not lagged behind many of the Pacific Rim countries now being generally admired. The trouble has been that consumption has outpaced growth, partly because of the exigencies of democratic politics and partly because of historically conditioned social habits. It need not always be so.

The acute phase of the Kurdish problem will probably continue. The policy of dealing with PKK terrorism by military means and of deferring political measures until the hoped-for day when terrorism will have been largely eliminated appears to enjoy the support of the majority of ethnic Turks. It is therefore likely that this policy will be applied either until it succeeds or until lack of success leads the Turkish public to change its mind. There is, of course, the danger that the attempt to solve the problem by military means alone will create ethnic hostility between Turks and Kurds where it does not exist today. But more likely the Turkish public, and the Turkish government that relies on it, will draw appropriate conclusions from recognizing the "Kurdish reality" that Süleyman Demirel acknowledged when he returned to office in December 1991.

Many Turkish commentators point out that the problem of terrorism should not be confused with the Kurdish problem. In Turkey as elsewhere, they say, there can be no compromise with terrorism. It must be fought. This is true, but still leaves open the question of what should be done to manage the Kurdish problem.

Foreign experience in dealing with ethnic divisions is relevant, but cannot be conclusive. Turkey will have to reach its own conclusions. The Kurdish problem is being debated in Turkey more widely and freely than ever before. Experience gained in implementing current policies will enrich this debate. Again, there is no reason to despair of a reasonable solution.

In the meantime, the outside world should not oversimplify the problem or ignore changes in attitudes. When the PKK terror campaign developed under the Motherland Party administration, an ethnic Kurd held the post of interior minister in Turkey. Today, for the first time, an ethnic Kurd is Turkish minister of foreign affairs. When President Süleyman Demirel states repeatedly, "I shall not allow the country to be broken up," one must assume that he means to do all he can to keep the Kurds within the Turkish polity. There will be no change in the goal of preserving Turkey one and undivided, but different paths can lead to it.

At the time of writing, the Turkish government has decided to suspend investment in the Kurdish areas for fear that money earmarked for development should end up in terrorist pockets. This is tantamount to abandoning, at least temporarily, the much-discussed economic solution to Kurdish disaffection. At present, because the military are

trying to defeat the terrorists, Turkish politicians are un-
willing to make proposals likely to stir up controversy
among ethnic Turks. But it seems that at least some of
them are considering long-term political strategies. Those
who wish to undermine Turkey as a regional power point
to the persistence of the Kurdish problem, or even try to
aggravate it.

No doubt the Kurdish problem is weakening Turkey
and restricting its ability to play a constructive role on the
wider international stage. But if the difficulties that Turkey is experiencing in making room for Kurdish aspirations
are limiting its strength, they do not negate it. Although
the West can properly criticize particular methods used by
the Turkish authorities to pacify the Kurdish areas, it must
beware of giving comfort to forces of disintegration. Their
threat is not limited to Turkey.

Whatever the outcome of its Kurdish troubles, Turkey
will continue to be a partner of the advanced industrialized
nations of the world, particularly the West. It shares the
West's interest in a stable, democratic world order, to
which the growing energies of its people can contribute.
This community of interests was demonstrated in the long
years of the cold war and more recently during the Gulf
War. In the fluid, uncertain situation that has followed,
Turkey and the West need each other as never before.
Clearly, world order cannot be ensured only by imposing
external force, but must rely on local resources of law and
order. Because Turkey is one such resource, its strength
and stability are in the Western interest. The West must of
course understand both Turkey's weaknesses and its
strengths. It must be frank with Turkish leaders, as Western leaders are frank with each other. But it must remain
determined to keep Turkey as a friend.

Notes

1. Justin McCarthy, *Muslims and Minorities: The Population of Ottoman Anatolia and the End of Empire* (New York: New York University Press, 1983), 138.

2. Feroz Ahmad, *The Making of Modern Turkey* (London: Routledge, 1993), 226.

3. Quoted in Suha Bolukbasi, *Turkish-American Relations and Cyprus* (Washington, D.C.: University Press of America, 1988), 77.

4. M. Ali Birand, *12 Eylül: Saat 04.00* [12 September: 04.00 Hours] (Istanbul: Karacan, 1984), 320.

5. General Secretariat of National Security Council, *12 September in Turkey: Before and After* (Ankara, 1982), 253–259.

6. Translated from text in Sabahattin Selek, *Millî Mücadele I: Anadolu Ihtilâli* [National Struggle I: The Anatolian Revolution] (Istanbul, 1963), 276.

7. For a full treatment of Kurdish linguistics, consult Amir Hassanpour, *Nationalism and Language in Kurdistan 1918–1985* (San Francisco: Mellen Research University Press, 1992).

8. Analysis of 1965 census by mother tongue is given in Geoffrey Lewis, *Modern Turkey* (London: Ernest Benn, 1974), 211–222.

9. Martin van Bruinessen, *Agha, Shaikh and State* (London: Zed Books, 1992), 14–15.

10. Figures from an unpublished paper by Cem Behar, "Tendances récentes de la population de la Turquie," presented at conference on "L'aire turque dans la nouvelle configuration régionale et internationale" (Ankara), November 2–3, 1992. Countrywide infant mortality figure from OECD Economic Surveys, *Turkey*, Paris, April 17, 1994, p. 66.

11. Robert Olson, *The Emergence of Kurdish Nationalism and the Sheikh Said Rebellion* (Austin: University of Texas Press, 1989), 39–41.

12. *Turkey Confidential* (London), December 1992, p. 8, quoting Interior Minister Ismet Sezgin.

13. *Milliyet* (Istanbul), August 3, 1993, p. 18.

14. OECD Economic Surveys, *Turkey* (Paris), August 3, 1992, p. 88.

15. Ibid., April 6, 1993, p. 59.

16. Ibid., 110.

17. [Turkish] State Institute of Statistics, *Temmuz 1993'de Türkiye Ekonomisi* [Turkish Economy in July 1993] (Ankara), p. Isgücü-3 [Labour-3].

18. Haluk Geray, "Turkey's Communications Boom," in *Turkish Review* (Ankara), Spring 1993, p. 26.

19. [Turkish] State Institute of Statistics, Press Release No. 64, June 25, 1993, concerning urban pollution during the winter of 1992–1993.

20. OECD statistics on the member countries, supplement to *OECD Observer* (Paris), June–July 1993, pp. 6–7.

21. The rise of the Sabanci dynasty is chronicled in Sadun Tanju (trans. Geoffrey Lewis), *The Life of Hacı Ömer Sabancı: The Turkish Village Boy Who Built an Industrial Empire* (Saffron Walden: World of Information, 1988).

22. *Temmuz 1993'de Türkiye Ekonomisi*, pp. HGTH-3, 4.

23. Translated from Rona Aybay, *Karşılastırmalı 1961 Anayasası* [Comparative (Text) of 1961 Constitution] (Istanbul: Fakültelerarası Matbaası, 1963), 6.

24. *Milliyet*, December 12, 1993, and January 30, 1992.

25. [Turkish] State Institute of Statistics, *1991 Statistical Yearbook of Turkey* (Ankara), November 1992, pp. 152, 154.

26. Nilüfer Narlı, "Radical Islamicism in Turkey and Its Political Implications: A Case Study of Turkish University Students" (Istanbul), November 20, 1992, unpublished survey report.

27. Text of letter in introduction to Turgut Ӧzal, *Turkey in Europe and Europe in Turkey* (Nicosia: K. Rustem, 1991).

28. OECD Economic Surveys, *Greece* (Paris), September 4, 1992, p. 40, table 10.

29. See György Hazai, "La question linguistique dans le monde turc actuel," in *CEMOTI* (Paris), no. 14 (1991): 6–11.

30. Text in *Newspot* (Ankara), 92/13, July 2, 1992.

Selected Bibliography

The standard historical work of reference is *History of the Ottoman Empire and Modern Turkey*, vol. 1, by Stanford J. Shaw (New York: Cambridge University Press, 1976), and vol. 2, by Stanford J. Shaw and Ezel Kural Shaw (New York: Cambridge University Press, 1977). The best account of the Turkish reforms is in Bernard Lewis, *The Emergence of Modern Turkey* (New York: Oxford University Press, 1961), which is supplemented by Niyazi Berkes, *The Development of Secularism in Turkey* (Montreal: McGill University Press, 1964). The work of these and other authors has been brought together and their narrative updated by Erik J. Zürcher in *Turkey: A Modern History* (London: I.B. Tauris, 1993). Readers in a hurry can turn to Roderic H. Davison, *Turkey: A Short History* (Walkington, England: Eothen Press, 1981). Lord Kinross's *Atatürk: The Rebirth of a Nation* (London: Weidenfeld & Nicolson, 1964), is still the best biography of the republic's founding father.

The political history of the Turkish republic to 1980 is covered in three books by C.H. Dodd: *Politics and Government in Turkey* (Manchester, England: Manchester University Press, 1969); *Democracy and Development in Turkey* (Walkington, England: Eothen Press, 1979); and *The Crisis of Turkish Democracy* (Walkington, England: Eothen Press, 1983). For an alternative view, turn to Feroz Ahmad, *The Turkish Experiment in Democracy 1950–1975* (London: Royal Institute of International Affairs, 1977), and *The Making of Modern Turkey* (London: Routledge,

1993). The interplay between politics and economics is explained in William Hale, *The Political and Economic Development of Modern Turkey* (London: Croom Helm, 1981). William Hale's *Turkish Politics and the Military* (London: Routledge, 1993) illuminates an important aspect of modern Turkish history.

Among one-volume introductions, the most recent and best are George S. Harris, *Turkey: Coping with Crisis* (Boulder, Colo.: Westview Press, 1985), and Dankwart A. Rustow, *Turkey: America's Forgotten Ally* (New York: Council on Foreign Relations, 1987).

The standard work on Turkish foreign policy is still Ferenc A. Váli, *Bridge across the Bosporus* (Baltimore: Johns Hopkins University Press, 1971), but look for a more up-to-date account about to be published by William Hale and Philip Robins (the latter is the author of *Turkey and the Middle East* (London: Royal Institute of International Affairs, 1991). In the meantime, there is much information to be gained from the essays edited by Graham E. Fuller and Ian O. Lesser in *Turkey's New Geopolitics: From the Balkans to Western China* (Boulder, Colo.: Westview Press, 1993). Readers interested in diplomatic history can turn to Selim Deringil, *Turkish Foreign Policy during the Second World War* (New York: Cambridge University Press, 1989), and memoirs such as George McGhee, *The U.S.-Turkish-NATO Middle East Connection* (London: Macmillan, 1990), and Parker T. Hart, *Two NATO Allies at the Threshold of War* (Durham: Duke University Press, 1990).

There is an extensive literature on Greek-Turkish relations and Cyprus. The most convenient introduction is Tozun Bahcheli, *Greek-Turkish Relations since 1955* (Boulder, Colo.: Westview Press, 1990), which provides an excellent bibliography for further study, but omits Suha Bolukbasi, *Turkish-American Relations and Cyprus* (Lanham, Md.: University Press of America, 1988.

In the controversy surrounding the past of Turkish-Armenian relations, the Turkish view is advanced by Kamuran Gürün, *The Armenian File* (Nicosia: Rustem, and London: Weidenfeld & Nicolson, 1985), and the Armenian side is championed by Christopher J. Walker, *Armenia: The Survival of a Nation* (London: Croom Helm, 1980). More recent events are covered by Michael M. Gunter, *"Pursuing the Just Cause of their People": A Study of Contemporary Armenian Terrorism* (Westport, Ct.: Greenwood, 1986).

Michael Gunter has also written two books about the Kurds: *The Kurds in Turkey: A Political Dilemma* (Boulder, Colo.: Westview Press, 1990), and *The Kurds of Iraq: Tragedy and Hope* (New York: St. Martin's Press, 1992). For historical background, consult Robert Olson, *The Emergence of Kurdish Nationalism and the Sheikh Said Rebellion, 1880–1925* (Austin: University of Texas Press, 1989. Mehrdad Izady, *The Kurds: A Concise Handbook* (Washington, D.C.: Crane Russak, 1992) illustrates the views of Kurdish nationalists.

On the fast-changing economic scene, begin with Anne Kruger and Okan Aktan, *Swimming against the Tide: Turkish Trade Reform in the 1980s* (San Francisco: Institute for Contemporary Studies, 1992) and go on to the annual country surveys published by the Organization for Economic Cooperation and Development in Paris. For many facts and figures in this book I am indebted to the Turkish State Institute of Statistics (SIS) in Ankara, which publishes a yearbook in Turkish and English (the last in my possession covers 1991 and was published in November 1992), and, in Turkish only, monthly surveys and more than a hundred press releases a year. Under its director, Professor Orhan Güvenen, the SIS has become an indispensable source of up-to-date accurate information on Turkey.

Index